Generation of Men

How to raise your son to be a healthy man among men

Clayton Lessor, PhD, LPC

THE
QUEST
PROJECT

Generation of Men

How to raise your son to be a healthy man among men
By Clayton Lessor, PhD, LPC
Quest Project Press

Published by: Quest Project Press, St. Louis, MO
Copyright ©2019 Clayton Lessor
All rights reserved.

Copyeditor: Nina Durfee, www.ninadurfee.com

Index: Elena Gwynne, www.quillandinkindexing.com

Cover Design: Tom Hudder, www.variomarketing.com

Interior Design: Davis Creative, www.daviscreative.com

ISBN: 978-0-9963607-3-9 (paperback)
        978-0-9963607-4-6 (Kindle)
        978-0-9963607-5-3 (ePub)

Library of Congress Number: 2018915092

Dedication

To generations of men

Past

Present

Future

Contents

Acknowledgments

Thank you to all the fathers who are doing their best to raise their sons to be responsible, strong and well-adjusted young men. It takes patience and wisdom that will be tested often.

I commend each of you, from the dad who's doing all the right things to the dad who is working hard to figure out what that is. Don't give up, your son needs you.

You compete every day with technology, electronics, and multiple attacks on what a male's role is in this society.

We are masculine, tender, strong, vulnerable, leaders, followers, intelligent, and we're not to be taken for granted! We're "a man among many!"

I hope you'll find this book useful in recalling what exactly it is a boy needs to become a man. You're the most important person in your son's life; that's an honor.

And…

Thank you to the entire team who made this book possible, it is truly a labor of love!

Introduction

America's boys are broken.

You see it in the headlines, week after week. Another school shooting. Another lonely, troubled teen losing hope and turning to violence. And for every dramatic incident you see on the nightly news, there are thousands of boys who are growing up lonely and alienated, falling behind their female peers, unsure of where they fit in in a world that suddenly regards the idea of masculinity as "toxic"—something dangerous that needs to be eliminated, like a disease.

Theories abound as to what's behind the trouble with our boys, from the absence of religion in home and at school to the proliferation of violent movies, TV shows, and video games. While those may be legitimate factors, after years of research and individual and group work as a psychotherapist who specializes in troubled boys, I believe there is another, much more powerful reason our boys are in crisis.

They are growing up without their fathers.

Whatever brought you here, the fact that you're taking the time to gain a deeper understanding of what your son is experiencing and how to help him means you're taking a step toward breaking this destructive cycle. By understanding what your son needs from you, and by learning to provide it for him, you will dramatically improve his chances of growing into a healthy, well-adjusted man. Not only that, you may also gain some clarity about your own boyhood, and why you are the man you are, both as a father and as a human being.

Still, if you're like most dads, you didn't pick up this book for you. You did it for your son—maybe because he's in trouble, or maybe because he seems withdrawn or unhappy, and you (or his mom) are worried and wondering what to do. Adolescence is a challenging time, and it's hard to know what you, as a father, should be doing to make sure your son doesn't slip through the cracks, to ensure he grows up to be a happy, healthy, productive citizen.

The most common question I hear from the fathers of sons is: *"How do I parent him?"*

How do you parent a teenage boy? And, if your son is in trouble, how can you help get him out of trouble and keep him from becoming another statistic? I wrote this book to answer those questions and to address some of the common issues boys experience during their teenage years. I also wrote it to help fathers gain a clearer picture of what their boys are going through by understanding their own experiences as men. This deeper level of understanding can help you build the kind of relationship with your son that will guide and support him through the rough patches, so he can become the man he's meant to be.

That's what being a parent—being a Good Dad—is all about.

Be assured that whatever your son is experiencing that brought you here, it's probably normal. The adolescent years have a bad reputation for good reason; the transition from childhood to adulthood is an emotional roller-coaster ride, even for the most well-adjusted kids (and parents!). But the expectation that raising a teenage son means Hell on Earth with a hip-hop (or death metal) soundtrack can actually be part of the problem. When a boy who has always seemed happy and well-adjusted starts behaving differently, it's hard to tell what's a real problem and what's "normal" teenage behavior. This uncertainty causes parents to put off seeking professional help, until things get so bad they no longer have a choice. That late in the game is when bad things start to happen.

Luckily, that's frequently the point where a parent—usually the mother—will take action and show up in my office with a boy who has always loved school but came home with a failing report card. Or a happy, mellow kid who has suddenly become angry, belligerent, or even aggressive. Or a young man who used to be popular and outgoing but has suddenly become sullen, depressed, and uncommunicative.

Getting help at this stage is crucial. Because what these parents—and you—may not realize is that, for every problem you notice, there are others that you are completely unaware of. Teenage boys are experts at hiding alcohol and drug use. They easily hide self-destructive or criminal behavior, like vandalism or shoplifting. They may also hide the fact that they feel lost or unhappy, or angry and desperate, or like they don't fit in. Would your son tell you if he was depressed, or even if he was contemplating suicide? Would you be able to figure it out on your own?

Maybe not. But the important thing for you to understand right now is that whatever problems your son is experiencing can be solved. And you are the key to solving them.

You have the power to break the cycle.

The relationship between a boy and his father is the most significant relationship in a boy's life. That relationship helps him figure out who he is and helps him decide who he wants to be. It teaches him what masculinity means, and it teaches him how to be a man. This book is designed to help you repair and grow your relationship with your son into one that is healthy and supports your son to reach his full potential.

I talk a lot about the importance of fathers in boys' lives. However, if you came to this book as a concerned stepfather, grandfather, uncle, or some other adult male who has taken over some of the father's traditional role, please keep reading. The boy you are reading this for needs you even more. This book will help you identify what he needs and offer some solutions to help you provide it.

Over the next few chapters, I'll share what I've learned about boys in more than two decades of professional practice, what our society has failed to give them, and why it's so hard for fathers to understand what their sons really need and how to provide it. I'll share the five essential things your son needs to become a man and some proven approaches and techniques that will help you make sure he gets that support. I'll help you gain a deeper understanding of your own experiences as a teenager and a man, so you can connect with your boy on a deeper level and establish the kind of relationship that will provide the foundation he needs to grow up healthy and happy.

Finally, I'll introduce you to a group of men who have experienced the same kinds of issues you and your son might be experiencing now. They'll share their stories of what they experienced, what they learned, how they healed, and where they and their sons are today. Together, we'll show you that, regardless of where he is or what he's experiencing at the moment, your son's future can be bright.

He just needs your help to get there.

CHAPTER 1

Meet Your Fantasy Son

I*t's a boy.*

Be honest. When you first heard those words, your heart probably stopped for a millisecond. Even if you were one of those guys who swore he would have been perfectly fine with a girl "as long as she's healthy," and all that politically correct B.S., deep down inside, you wanted a boy. Even if you weren't in your child's mother's life anymore, the knowledge that somewhere out there you had your own, personal mini-me was a powerful feeling.

Having a son can feel almost like getting a do-over. All the mistakes you made, all the stupid things you did when you were growing up, your boy's not going to do that. He's going to have a leg up on the competition, because unlike you, or maybe like you, he's going to do this life thing right. He's going to be the kid you wished you had been. He's going to be a winner.

Because he's your fantasy son.

As a therapist, let me first reassure you that there's nothing abnormal about creating your own, imaginary, perfect child in your head. Every parent has hopes and dreams for their children—not just dads; moms too. You look at your newborn boy and see endless possibilities. Will he be a doctor? A star athlete? Head of a corporation? President of the United States?

The problem with this kind of thinking is that there is usually—in fact, always—a difference between this fantasy son you've created in your mind and the actual, flesh-and-blood child you have in real life. So I developed this exercise to get parents thinking about the difference between their expectations for their children and the reality of who those children are.

Take a few minutes to fill it out here—you'll need a piece of paper and a pen.

Part 1

Think about the child you saw in your mind when you first heard the words, "It's a boy." At this beginning moment of his life, who did you dream that boy would be? A straight-A student? The captain of the football team? Class president? Would he help out around the house or in the backyard or do his homework without complaining? Would he be smart, funny, talented, ambitious, athletic, or charming? What would his friends be like? What would your relationship be with him? How would his life unfold?

Write all those things down, and anything else that comes to mind. Fill at least half a page to a page. There are no wrong answers, there's no good or bad here. As I said before, this fantasizing is normal. All parents have dreams and expectations for their children. Now is the time to write them down and acknowledge them.

Finished? Now comes the hard part.

Take that piece of paper, and everything it represents, and throw it away. You can burn it, put it through a shredder, tear it into little pieces, feed it to your dog, whatever works. Because, as you probably already know, that fantasy son does not exist.

But don't feel too bad. You probably aren't the parent your son fantasizes about either.

The process of destroying this "fantasy son" may spark a reaction, like sadness or anger. That's completely normal. It's normal to grieve for the son you dreamed of raising but never had. You're letting go of something that may be more important to you than you realize, even if it is only a fantasy.

If you need to, take some time to process whatever you're feeling, provided you don't take it out on your son or another human being or the family dog. Then, when you're ready, come back to this book.

Part 2

For the second half of the exercise, take another piece of paper and write a new list, this time of things you know about the son you have today. Try to answer the same questions you did in the first part. Who is this boy at this moment in his life? What sort of things does he do? What are his strengths? His weaknesses? What is his life like? Write both the bad and the good things. Again, try to fill at least a half a page. And be honest—this exercise was designed to help you and your son. There's no judgment involved, so write everything you know is true.

Now, review the list. It may be significantly different from the first list, and if that's the case, you did it right. The first list you made wasn't worth much, which is why I had you throw it away. But this new list has the power to help you and your son move forward.

For example, you'll probably see your son's problem behavior on this new list (and if you don't, go back and add it). From now on, you'll remember not to be surprised by that behavior, because you have acknowledged it and identified it on your list. Now all that's left is to deal with it by figuring out where you need to set boundaries and what solutions will encourage your son to respect those boundaries.

You should also see some of your son's good qualities on that list. If not, go back and add at least three good qualities. This is critically important, because, by acknowledging and identifying these good qualities, you give yourself and your son a starting place for the journey ahead. When you start by looking for and focusing on the things about your son that are good and positive, you put yourself in a place of support and appreciation for the real, unique, flesh-and-blood human being your child is.

Moving Forward

I designed this exercise to bring parents like you into the present moment. By letting go and grieving the child you never had, you can stop forcing the child you do have to fit the mold of your fantasy son, the one you invented before you had any idea what parenting was all about. Now you can begin to see your child for the person he truly is, you can learn to appreciate his unique gifts, and you can focus on how to help him grow and thrive.

Stop dreaming about who you want your son to be. Help him become the healthy, happy, and successful man he's meant to be.

Let's get started.

CHAPTER 2

The Problem with Punishment

How do you handle your son's misbehavior?

Chances are good that you're reading this book because your son did something that you (or his mother, or his teacher, or someone else in authority) didn't want him to do. All children, male and female, are guilty of occasional "bad" behavior, because testing boundaries and breaking rules is one of the ways they learn and grow. Unfortunately, dealing with that type of learning and growing is never easy for parents, and figuring out the best way to handle that very normal behavior (as well as more extreme, less normal versions of that behavior) can be like traversing a minefield.

A lot of fathers have no idea how to respond when their boy does something that's against the rules, especially if those rules were never clearly established in the first place. When their son comes home with a bad report card, gets in a fight, or is caught drinking or smoking a cigarette, they know they're supposed to do *something*. They just don't know what that something is.

A Brief History of Punishment

When I was growing up in the 1960s, there wasn't a lot of confusion over what to do with a misbehaving child. When I was caught doing something I wasn't supposed to do, I was spanked. The thing is, my father got physically violent whenever he was upset about anything, so getting hit when I was "bad" didn't mean much to me; I would no doubt be hit again at some point when I was being "good." Still, most of my friends also received spankings when they misbehaved. "Spare the rod, spoil the child" was the common wisdom at the time, and spanking was viewed as an unpleasant—but necessary and normal—part of parenting.

Today, that view no longer prevails, at least not in the psychological community. Decades of research has determined that spanking not only damages kids psychologically, it simply doesn't work as a tool to modify a child's behavior. That's why the American Psychological Association recommends that "parents and caregivers reduce and potentially eliminate their use of any physical punishment as a disciplinary method" and asks psychologists and other professionals to "indicate to parents that physical punishment is not an appropriate, or even a consistently effective, method of discipline."

Spanking has also fallen out of favor around the world in general. In 2006, The United Nations Committee on the Rights of the Child called physical punishment "legalized violence against children" that should be eliminated in all settings. One hundred ninety-two countries signed on to the treaty. At this writing, at least thirty countries around the world have completely banned physical punishment of children.

The United States, however, is not one of those countries.

The USA was one of only two nations that failed to ratify that U.N. treaty, in part because (according to surveys) the majority of Americans still believe that physical punishment is an acceptable form of discipline. If you are one of them, I'm not here to judge you. However, I will be presenting you with a more effective alternative to physical punishment later in this chapter.

Modern Punishment

Most of the boys I see in my practice do not receive spankings—at least not by the time they get to me. When I ask a new boy, "When's the last time you got hit?"

the standard answer is that he was seven or eight the last time he was spanked or slapped or that mom or dad "used the belt" on him. This could be because parents today know that they're risking a meeting with DFS (the Department of Family Services) if they're caught physically disciplining their child. Spanking may not be illegal, but child abuse is, and the line between the two isn't always clear.

With spanking off the table, many of today's fathers don't know what to do when their children get in trouble. I can't tell you how many dads just ignore their sons' bad behavior and hope it will go away, or leave the discipline for Mom to handle. Other dads will give their sons a "talking to"—spending what seems like hours explaining why the thing their child did was wrong and why they should never, ever do it again. While that impulse to talk things through is positive, it isn't especially effective. Boys don't have the attention span to absorb and benefit from all that information. If you talk for more than five minutes about anything other than video games or sports, they shut down.

That's not rudeness, it's just biology.

Still, most of the fathers I see feel the need to "do something" about their child's misbehavior, and in their minds, that usually means administering some form of punishment. They believe the only way to stop a child from breaking the rules is to inflict pain on him in order to send a message that he shouldn't break that rule again and will suffer if he does. Punishment usually takes the form of "grounding"—I work with some kids who it seems must be grounded for life—or taking away privileges like cell phones, video games, and other toys. Punishments like these are extremely common. They also don't work any better than spanking.

You may have already learned this through trial and error with your own son. What you may not yet know is the reason *why* the whole concept of "punishment" doesn't work. *It's because punishment isn't really about your boy. It's about you.*

Punishment offers instant gratification for angry parents. It happens in the moment when you're upset and you want to convey to your son that he did something wrong and cause enough pain that he will remember and not do that thing again. So you do something to make him feel as bad as you feel, or even worse, and after that you think your job is done.

But it isn't, because your child doesn't really learn anything from the experience.

Well, that's not entirely true. He learns to be afraid of getting caught, but that's not a lesson you want to teach. It can actually make the behavior worse, pushing it underground and teaching your son to become a better liar, a better sneaker, better at finding ways to keep doing what he's doing without getting caught.

Do you feel like you're running out of options? If punishment doesn't work, and hitting doesn't work, and talking doesn't work, but at the same time you're not supposed to ignore your child's bad behavior, what else can you do?

That's easy. You can provide discipline.

Discipline vs. Punishment

A lot of parents believe that spanking and grounding are forms of discipline, but that's not true. In fact, discipline and punishment are two completely different concepts. The word *discipline* is derived from the root word *discere,* which means "to learn." When you discipline a child, the goal is not to inflict physical or emotional discomfort, but to teach him something by employing what we call *natural consequences.*

A natural consequence is something that automatically happens as a result of something else, like getting a sunburn when you forget to wear sunscreen or getting a bad grade when you don't study for a test. Of course, your son's behavior might not automatically produce such a clear, natural consequence quite like that—if he's smoking cigarettes, he may get cancer in thirty or forty years, but he probably won't get it at age fourteen. So, it's your job as a parent to create natural consequences that will deliver the lesson your son needs to learn *now*.

First, a caveat. If your son is doing drugs or drinking, and it's chronic and habitual, now is not the time to employ natural consequences. It's time to get him to a treatment center. He may be experiencing some natural consequences from his behavior already, like falling grades; but if he's addicted to a substance, those consequences won't have much of an effect. Addiction is too powerful for that. It's important for your child to be treated by experts in substance abuse and addiction first, to get that problem under control. Once the addiction has been dealt with and your son has been given the tools to cope, you can address the underlying causes of his behavior.

On the other hand, if your son is experimenting with the occasional beer or hit off a vaporizer, or if his behavior is more about things like bad grades, skipping chores, fighting, or talking back, natural consequences are the best discipline. This isn't rocket science. Don't overthink it; trust the process!

Using natural consequences requires being proactive and dealing with problem behavior *before* it happens, by sitting down with your son and laying down the rules of the house in advance. Tell him, "These are the rules. If you follow these rules, you get to do what you want, within reason." Then comes the important part. Ask your child, "What is it that you want?" Believe me, he'll tell you.

Like most teenage boys, your son probably has an almost endless list of things he wants you to buy for him or let him do. As long as your son follows the rules you've established in advance, natural consequences means he gets to do and have those things, provided they're age-appropriate, within reason, and you approve of them. You can even set up natural consequences to prevent behavior that you want to extinguish *and* reward behavior you want to encourage.

The trick to the whole thing is that, no matter what happens, you don't punish your son for his mistakes. You don't take anything away, ever. What you tell your son is, "You get to choose to have what you want or to not have what you want," and the way he makes that choice is by choosing to follow the rules. This takes you out of the way, because making it all about you instead of your son is what gets everybody in trouble in the first place. Giving your child responsibility for his behavior may not sound like an earth-shattering concept, but it does have earth-shattering effects when it comes to dealing with problem behaviors.

Establishing natural consequences lets your son feel his power. It puts him in control of what happens in his life and whether or not he gets what he wants. He'll reach a point where he's tempted to step the wrong way, and he'll suddenly remember, "Oops, I should have made a right instead of a left, and now I've got to understand the consequences for that." Once he breaks a rule, there is no question about what happens next.

With natural consequences, good behavior no longer means avoiding getting caught by Mom or Dad. It means making a conscious choice to step in the right direction. It's about learning the rules and learning that if he keeps doing what he's doing and following those rules, he'll get more of what he wants. As he continues to step into his power over the years and earns more and more of those things he wants, he'll understand how much control he has over what happens in his life. This helps him grow into a healthy, confident person who can go out into the world and do good work.

And isn't that exactly what you want?

Remember, natural consequences are an effective tool, but when you're establishing them for the first time, remember your son's attention span. Drone on for more than five minutes, and your son may forget ninety percent of what you say. Instead, make it a visual and physical thing. Use whiteboards, use charts, use anything that allows your son to visually and physically track his progress (or lack of it) and actually see where he's succeeding and where he's falling short. Then there's no begging you for the thing he wants. All he has to do is look at the chart to see if he's earned it. Boys respond well to that visual and physical effect, because the visual itself is rewarding.

And rewarding—not punishing—is the most effective kind of discipline.

CHAPTER 3

When to Contact the Authorities

I hope you will never be in a position where you need to consider calling the police or mental health authorities to help you help your son. But in this age of opioid abuse, school shootings, and other crises affecting our youth, the topic of "when to get help and how" needs to be addressed. Learn to recognize the signs that your son has become a danger to himself or others and know what to do next. This chapter will help you identify those signs and explain what actions you can take to avert a potential tragedy, from boundary-setting and parental intervention to calling 9-1-1.

This is a sensitive area for many parents, especially for Mom. No one wants to call the police or the mental health authorities and report that their child is out of control. Some don't even want to make an appointment with a therapist or talk to a school counselor. Don't get stuck in denial, ignoring red flags and justifying problem behavior until it's too late. Don't struggle for years to help your son without getting to the bottom of the problem.

When a boy reaches what appears to be a crisis point, you need to make a decision.

Involving the police or mental health officials in your family's personal business might sound undesirable and unnecessary, for a wide variety of reasons. If it turns out nothing is wrong, you'll look like you "overreacted" and wasted first responders' time. If there is a real problem, you will be on record as having "failed" as a father. Not only that, there may be long-term consequences for your son. Will he have a record? Will other people find out about it? Will it affect his chances of getting into college or getting a good job?

If you dial 9-1-1, are you at risk of ruining your son's life?

I promise you: No. In fact, you may be saving his life.

Bottom line, if you have any reason to fear that your son is a danger to himself or others, safety—your child's and that of those around him—needs to be your first and only priority. Call 9-1-1 immediately, or, if it's feasible, put your son in the car and drive him to a hospital or police station.

How to Tell if Your Child is Suicidal or Homicidal

In the absence of a "crisis point," it can be difficult to tell the difference between a teenager who is reacting normally to the emotional ups and downs of adolescence and one who may be on the path to hurting himself or someone else. However, there are some common signs most suicidal and homicidal teens exhibit that parents should learn to watch for.

According to the Jason Foundation, an organization that provides curriculum to schools, parents, and other teens about how teen suicide can be prevented, four out of five teens who attempt suicide give clear warning signs, including (but not limited to):

1. Talking about suicide

2. Making statements about feeling hopeless, helpless, or worthless

3. A deepening depression

4. Preoccupation with death

5. Taking unnecessary risks or exhibiting self-destructive behavior

6. Out-of-character behavior

7. A loss of interest in the things he cares about

8. Visiting or calling people he cares about

9. Making arrangements; setting his affairs in order

10. Giving away prized possessions

Teens who are considering violence against others exhibit many of the same warning signs, including depression and withdrawing from others. According to *Psychology Today*, teens who may be considered "dangerous" may also:

1. Have a previous history of violence, especially if the behavior is escalating

2. Abuse animals or other children

3. Show no empathy for others

4. Have a fascination with guns, knives, or other weapons, or violent media

5. Draw pictures or create other art depicting violence

6. Start fires

7. Share plans to hurt or kill another person

Before we go any further, I want to be clear. If your son exhibits some of the behaviors listed above, it doesn't necessarily mean he's headed for trouble. There are plenty of boys who start fires or play violent video games without harming another person. If every teenager who ever sulked alone in his room killed himself, few people would live to see their twentieth birthday. As a father, the key is to know your son. Keep your eyes on him, use common sense, and if you ever suspect that your son is suicidal or homicidal, don't wait. Call 9-1-1 or drive him to the hospital or police station and get him the help he needs. His life, or someone else's, may depend on it.

If You're Concered Your Son Will Hurt Himself

If you think your son may be suicidal, or if he is threatening to hurt himself, don't try to determine whether he's serious or just trying to get attention. Go straight to the hospital.

I believe you should treat cutting the same way. A boy is not going to die from a cut on his arm, but in my experience, boys use cutting as a game to get attention. If you don't want your son to cut himself to get attention (and trust me, you don't), treat the incident seriously. Take him to the hospital for an evaluation. Give him a clear message that self-harm is serious and, as his father, you will not allow him to hurt himself.

If you're worried that your son is suicidal, you may have no idea what to say or do. Take control of the situation by sitting down with your son and clearly walking him through the series of steps you are prepared to take to help him get better. Explain that you will start with counseling, and if that doesn't work, you will put him in an in-patient program. If that isn't enough, you will put him in a residential program. Emphasize that you will go as far as you need to help him get better.

By that point, a boy who is not serious about harming himself usually stops talking about suicide. If the talk continues, you know what to do. Follow through on the groundwork you laid and get him the help he needs.

If Your Son is Violent

If your son shows aggression toward you or his mother, act immediately. The moment when a parent feels threatened by his child is a sign that misbehavior has gone too far. This is where domestic violence begins, and it is your responsibility to stop it in its tracks.

Start by Setting the Ground Rules

Employ the "natural consequences" method of discipline I described earlier. Set boundaries and put those consequences in place. In many cases, the existence of rules, the knowledge that they will be enforced, and an incentive for doing well is enough to help a boy get problem behavior under control. Of course, this is contingent on your being consistent. Remember, when he breaks the rules, you don't yell, you don't lecture, you don't threaten. You simply employ the consequence and move on.

Raise the Stakes

If natural consequences fail to stop your son's problem behavior, it's time to introduce a new, stronger consequence. Tell your son that if he does not improve, you will bring in outside help. If he's never seen a counselor or therapist before, that could be the consequence (although I like to think of myself as something more than a consequence!). If he's already in counseling, the consequence could be a local in-patient program. Whatever consequence you choose, remember: you must follow through, or your son will recognize what you say as an empty threat, and the problem behavior will get even worse.

The Scare Tactic

The scare tactic is slightly controversial, but I recommend it for boys who continue their problem behavior even when the consequences have been increased. It's not easy, but I promise it works—probably because it's harsh. And sometimes, being harsh now can help you avoid bigger problems down the line.

Call your local police station and arrange to meet (without your son) with the "relationship officer"—the cop who basically serves as the department's representative in your community. Tell the relationship officer about the problems you are having with your son, and ask this officer, or any willing male officer, to have a "scared straight" conversation with your son. Keep in mind this will only work if the issue is serious enough to be "intervention worthy," like if your son is threatening violence.

For a boy who is becoming a danger to himself or others, police are specifically trained to handle interventive interactions. They know how to tell a boy that if he continues to threaten people, or hurts anyone, "I'm going to come with the handcuffs and put you in the back of the car, and you will sit in a cell." They speak in a way that your son will probably take very seriously. It may sound dramatic, but that kind of drama is exactly what a boy who is threatening violence needs to hear.

Follow Through

One visit from the police is usually enough to scare any kid straight. But if your son does not respond, if his bad behavior continues, follow through. Call the police officer and tell him you need him to come back and do what he said he would do. Remember, police are trained for these situations, and the officer will come to you with a plan.

The cop will come to your house, go through the process of arresting and handcuffing your son, and put him in the back of the police car. The officer will get in the car with your son and talk to him about his behavior and the potential consequences. At the end of the conversation, instead of taking your son to the police station for booking, the officer will tell him he's getting another chance. He will deliver your son back to your door, shaken, but hopefully ready to turn over a new leaf.

It is a little harsh. But in my experience, the best way to get ahead of a serious problem with your son is by demonstrating you are serious. Just remember, follow-through is imperative There's no better way to ensure your son ends up in jail than to continually threaten to call the cops without ever following through.

Extra Help

No matter how dedicated you are to your son's well-being, no matter how many things you try, you may reach a point where there is nothing more you can do for your son. Please note that this is extremely rare if you follow the other steps in this book. However, if it's still the case, know that an in-patient program can offer hope. The right in-patient program can give your son exactly what he needs to overcome his problems and return to his normal life with a fresh start.

If you think in-patient care is the solution for your son, start your research now. Talk to doctors, counselors, and other parents about their experiences and who they recommend. Educate yourself about your options and work with a counselor you trust to come up with a plan.

It's only too late if you give up. Don't give up.

CHAPTER 4

The Wound All Boys (and Men) Share

The age of eleven or twelve is pivotal for boys, because that's when their bodies and their minds begin to send them signals that things are changing. It can be almost like a switch that flips, and suddenly, they don't want to spend all their time by their mother's side anymore. When a boy starts to transition into adolescence, he starts looking for his dad. Think back. I bet you remember exactly what I'm talking about.

For most of human history, Dad wasn't very hard to find. A boy would stay close to his mother when he was little and needed constant care, eventually graduating to learning some basic skills and doing simple chores around the house. But when that boy reached the age of eleven or twelve, the job of raising him automatically passed from his mother to his father. We've seen this as far back as the early Greeks, who taught their sons how to farm the land and even, when the time called for it, how to be warriors. For hundreds of years, the trend continued; farmers took their sons into the fields, shopkeepers took their sons to the shop, even doctors' sons accompanied their fathers on their rounds.

That was the way boys learned to be men.

It continued from generation to generation, as fathers passed their wisdom—which they gained from their own fathers—down to their sons. Working together side by side, for weeks, months, and eventually years, a father would gradually and almost effortlessly transfer everything he knew to his child, actively helping to shape the man he would become. There was never any question about the need to be "present" or "available" to his child, because the survival of the family and, on a larger scale, the society, depended on it. Children needed to become contributing members of their households and communities as quickly as possible, so they learned how to set goals and meet them, how to take responsibility, and what it meant to work hard. They also learned to handle the inevitable ups and downs of life—things like conflict, failure, disappointment, and struggle—first by observing how their fathers did it, and later when their fathers helped guide them through their own issues. By the time a boy reached his late teens, he had all the tools he needed to go out on his own and succeed as a man.

But the industrial revolution changed all that. Suddenly, men had options beyond staying in the same town where they'd always lived and following in their fathers' footsteps. Now they had choices. They could pursue a different type of work or leave home to seek their fortunes. As a result, fathers started moving farther and farther away from their homes and, as a consequence, from their sons. They moved off the farms and out of the local shops to the offices and factories, or even to the road, if their work required it.

At the end of the day, when these dads came home from the factory or the shop or the road, the last thing they wanted to do was dedicate more time to transferring their knowledge to their sons. It's still true today. After dealing with whatever stress you have to cope with at work all day and fighting traffic all the way home, you probably don't have the time or the energy to teach your son the things he might be missing while you're away doing your job. More likely, you come home and say, "I just gotta sit in my recliner and pop my feet up and watch TV so I can do it all over again tomorrow"—if you even have time for that.

The result is, while you might think you're simply doing what you have to do to get by and support your family, at the same time, you're part of this cycle. You're depriving your son of the guidance he needs. But don't feel too guilty, because you're not alone. The average amount of time an American father spends one-on-one with his son today is ten minutes. A week. (Yes, this is a documented fact.)

For the sons of these fathers, what's left in place of that time with their dads and the relationship that would otherwise develop over years of close contact is emptiness.

That's the wound all boys share. It's a wound most men share.

Even you.

The Absent Father

I call this phenomenon "The Absent Father," and it's been building for generations to become a systemic problem affecting a large number of our boys today. It's epidemic in every region of the country and exists in every part of the economic spectrum. It's essentially the way life *is*.

The majority of boys I see in my practice have a father who is *physically* absent, meaning he is not living in the home with his son. With half of all marriages ending in divorce, and less traditional parenting arrangements gaining acceptance and becoming more common, two-parent families are no longer the norm in our society. And ironically, despite all this progress toward gender equality, when it comes to who gets custody of the kids in divided families, not only does society seem to favor the mother, the court system does as well.

If you're a non-custodial father, your relationship with your son may depend on what kind of relationship you have with his mom.

Some moms and dads handle separation well. They put aside any bad feelings that might linger from their relationship for the good of their kids, and they work together as a team to find healthy ways to co-parent. However, parents are human. In some human relationships, parents' tensions can build to the point where they spill over into their interactions with their kids. This can take the form of anything from arguments over where kids spend the holidays, to cancelled visits with Dad, to an actual psychological disorder called Parental Alienation Syndrome, in which a child is systematically convinced by one parent to hate the other.

In other words, if you're a non-custodial dad, maintaining regular contact with your son can be challenging. In some cases, it feels impossible. If your boy is having problems in school or with friends or even with the law, you might feel powerless to do anything about it. You might not even be aware that these things are happening in the first place.

Unfortunately, aware or not, research has determined that the growing number of Absent Fathers is having a negative effect on our society. Estimates say one in three boys currently lives in a home without a father or other strong male role model. The result is a generational crisis.

Studies show that boys who grow up without fathers are at a significant disadvantage. The simple fact that their father doesn't live with them makes them more likely than their peers to drop out of school, get involved in gangs, have trouble with the law, and experiment with drugs and alcohol.

I know this to be true, not only from my own research, but from personal experience. I see it in my practice all the time. You may have witnessed some (or all) of those behaviors in your own son, or he may be acting out without your even knowing.

Studies also show that boys who grow up without fathers are dramatically more likely to get into serious trouble. For example:

- 70% of adolescent boys in residential treatment centers are fatherless

- 72% of juveniles in state reform institutions grew up without parents or in single-parent homes

- 72% of adolescent murderers grew up without fathers

And, most shocking,

- More than 75% of all crime in America is committed by men who were fatherless as children

If your son is growing up without you, these statistics are less than welcome news. No one wants his child to have fewer options simply because of living arrangements. That's not exactly fair. But the fact that you're reading this book indicates that you haven't given up. The next step is to find a way to be present in your son's life, no matter what it takes. It may not be easy, and it may even require legal intervention if his mother refuses to cooperate. Keep trying, even if it feels impossible. Your son's future is worth fighting for, and he needs you in his future.

The Emotionally Absent Father

If you live under the same roof as your son, you may be breathing a sigh of relief, assuming the bad news above doesn't apply to you or your child. True, your son does gain an advantage simply by having you around. But don't pat yourself on the back just yet. A father doesn't have to live apart from his son to be an Absent Father. In many families the father is physically present, living in the same house as his son, acting as the head of the household, but for whatever reason, his mind and his energy are somewhere else. These men have mentally checked out, and their boys (and their partners) are suffering for it.

These are *emotionally* Absent Fathers, and they fall into a few distinct categories.

The Father Who Never Grew Up

Do you think of yourself as your son's buddy? Are you always available to take him out four-wheeling or fishing or golfing or on a trip to Disneyland or to the movies or whatever you like to do, but never seem to have time for his parent-teacher conferences? Will you spend hours playing video games or watching football with your son, only to disappear when something less fun, like making sure his homework gets done or confronting him about the bag of marijuana Mom found in his sock drawer, needs to be addressed? If so, you could be a Father Who Never Grew Up.

These fathers are present for their sons, but not in the way a father should be. Their relationships with their boys are more like that of an older brother, or maybe a fun uncle. They spend time with their sons, which is a good, positive thing, and it does produce some positive results. However, they still somehow fail to provide the guidance, the teaching, and the discipline an adolescent boy needs in order to become a responsible man. And that's the most important thing a father can provide to his son. As a dad, that's your job.

If your own father was a Dad Who Never Grew Up, or really any kind of Absent Father, you may have no idea what your son is supposed to learn from you (let alone how to teach him those things), because no one taught them to you. If your mom was always the person who made you do your homework and talked with your teachers, you may see these things as his mother's job. You weren't a part of that chain of wisdom—of knowledge passed down from father to son—because it was broken before you were born. This is your chance to rebuild that chain, beginning by strengthening the bond between you and your son. Later in this book we'll look at how.

The Incapacitated Father

People who are struggling with addiction or who have a history of abuse find it difficult to be present for anyone but themselves. Fathers with this history and experience almost automatically become Absent Fathers, because they are mentally incapable of providing the kind of steady, reliable presence their boy needs, even if they want to. The same can be true for a father suffering from severe depression—when it's hard to get out of bed in the morning, it's hard to consider and deal with the needs of another human being. Even physical conditions like Parkinson's disease or cancer can leave a father unable to do the basic work of parenting. If you are not well, "being there" for your son is a struggle, no matter how much you want to be.

This is not a criticism or a judgment. The fact that you're here despite falling into this category of Absent Father shows that, regardless of your circumstances, you have begun taking steps to be more involved in your son's life and development. This book won't cover everything you need to do to succeed despite your specific situation, but it will provide you with a roadmap for building a healthy relationship with your son, as well as some insight into how to heal your own psychological wounds. Please consider getting whatever other help you need to fully heal. You deserve it, and so does your son.

The Distracted Dad

At this point, you may be thinking, "None of this applies to me." Maybe your family is a picture-perfect, TV sitcom-worthy group where everything looks perfectly *normal*. You may coach Little League or volunteer as a Boy Scout leader or sit down at the table for dinner with the family every night, or even all of the above. But if your son is struggling, there's still a chance that, despite all the things you're doing right, you may be the type of Absent Father I call the Distracted Dad.

Distracted Dads tend to be workaholic, perfectionist types who are too busy, stressed out, and wrapped up in their own lives and problems to take the time to provide the hands-on guidance their sons need. They feel fine leaving most of the parenting to Mom, since they see it as her job, or at least as a job she's more suited to than they are. They feel confident that they're contributing everything they need to by working hard and doing what they can at home and with their kids (at least in their own minds). The problem is that, while they may be consistently physically present in their sons' lives, emotionally they are somewhere else.

Could this apply to you, even if you think you're a pretty good dad? There's an easy way to determine whether or not you are giving your son the amount of attention and guidance he needs and deserves.

Take a moment to think about the last week, leading up to right now. How much time did you spend with your son—not in a group setting, like as his soccer coach or at the dinner table with the whole family, but one on one. Write down every instance where you spent time alone with your son. Now add all the time together and see what you end up with.

If you didn't spend at least three hours of one-on-one time with your son, taking care of things that need to get done, sharing experiences you both enjoy, or even just hanging out, your son is not getting enough quality time with you in his life. You qualify as an Absent Father.

Ready to fix it?

CHAPTER 5

Who (and What) is Influencing Your Son?

Before we get into some of the ways you can build a stronger relationship with your boy, it's important to understand the forces that currently shape his behavior. We've established that the average American dad spends only ten minutes a week with his son. That means your child is spending upwards of 10,070 minutes a week with people and things that are Not You. As you might expect, those people and things have a powerful impact on your son's life and his world during what is an especially critical point in his development. They may also be influencing him in ways that you don't like or agree with.

Let's take a look at these influencers one at a time.

School

After his mother and immediate family, your son's school is probably the biggest influence in his life. Most kids spend about thirty hours every week in the school environment, so the teachers and administrators who are there to teach your son what he needs to know are in a position to have a major impact on him. Unfortunately, in today's education system, the mere fact that your son is your son—as opposed to your daughter—may have him at a disadvantage.

In the decades since Title IX passed back in 1972, schools have focused more attention and energy on girls. This is not a bad thing—girls and their abilities were overlooked for decades, so making sure they have a chance to play sports if they want to, are encouraged to excel in math and science, and are valued for more than their appearance and "helpfulness" are all positives. The problem is that, while there is this tremendous amount of focus on the needs of girls and how to help them succeed, the pendulum has swung so far in their direction that boys seem to have been forgotten. And, as the statistics show, boys are suffering for it.

Standardized tests indicate that boys and girls start out with intelligence and abilities that are basically equal. However, research shows that equal potential has not been translating into equal performance. Specifically, boys:

- Have significantly higher rates of learning disabilities

- Receive up to 70% of Ds and Fs given to all students

- Create 90% of all classroom discipline problems

- Have lower grade point averages than girls

- Are more likely to drop out of high school than girls

- Are less likely to graduate high school than girls

- Are less likely to go to college than girls

- Go on to earn fewer advanced degrees than their female counterparts

What that means is that whatever inequality (real or perceived) our education system was trying to correct back in the 1970s has now been overcorrected. Today, it's our boys who need special attention, and for the most part, they're not getting it.

Why is this happening? Why are our schools failing to serve our boys?

One problem may be that, even today, most teachers are female and may relate more to the female mindset. Girls are wired differently than boys. They're less likely to talk back or misbehave and more likely to stay on task, not because they're better human beings, but because of simple biology. In fact, five out of six children who are sent to see the doctor for Attention Deficit Disorder (ADD) or Attention Deficit Hyperactivity Disorder (ADHD) are boys, often simply for exhibiting typical male behavior their teachers may not like or understand (remember my earlier comments about a boy's attention span—those comments apply about school as well).

Teachers and administrators refer boys to doctors with the hope that those doctors will put them on medication, and that medication will make them behave more like the girls do. As a result, we're creating a generation of boys who are growing up medicated and suffering the side-effects of those medications, many of them unnecessarily.

What You Should Know about ADD/ADHD Medications

Overprescribing of ADD and ADHD medications is epidemic. I have worked with hundreds of school-aged boys over the years, and most of them walk into my office under the influence of at least one ADD or ADHD drug, if not some combination of drugs. Their stories follow a similar pattern:

1. A boy has problems in school.

2. His teacher or counselor suggests his parents talk to his doctor.

3. The doctor prescribes ADD or ADHD medication.

This is not only the doctor's fault. Physicians are trained to look for the most expedient medical solution to a problem, whether that problem is allergies or depression. They're not trained in psychology—things like analyzing behavior or teaching people to modify that behavior. Medications are their primary tool to treat a wide range of conditions, and ADD and ADHD are no exception. A pill is likely the best, easiest option they have available.

But that doesn't mean it's the best option for your son.

Many parents assume a prescription from a doctor is a "magic bullet" that will automatically make their child's symptoms disappear. In fact, medication only works on about fifty percent of ADHD cases. This could be because many kids diagnosed with ADD or ADHD don't have the condition in the first place. Most of the behaviors associated with these conditions can be linked to other factors, including depression, post-traumatic stress disorder (PTSD) (which we'll address a little later), and even environmental factors like instability or stress in the home environment. When those underlying factors are treated and dealt with, the ADD or ADHD symptoms often disappear.

Medications, on the other hand, treat only the symptoms—the behavior—and often not very well. In addition, medications frequently cause side effects, some of which are worse than the behavior the medication is prescribed to correct. In his book, *The ADD Answer: How to Help Your Child Now,* Dr. Frank Lawlis listed the most common side effects associated with ADD and ADHD medications. They are:

- Nervousness

- Insomnia

- Confusion

- Depression

- Agitation

- Irritability

- Stunted growth and development

He also lists less-common side effects including:

- Hyperactivity

- Hypersensitivity (allergy-type reactions to environmental agents)

- Anorexia

- Nausea

- Dizziness

- Heart palpitations

- Headaches

- Dyskinesia (movement-of-the-body problems)

- Drowsiness

- Hypertension (high blood pressure)

- Tachycardia (rapid, racing heartbeat)

- Angina (heart pain)

- Arrhythmia (heart rate changes)

- Abdominal Pain

- Lowered threshold for seizures

Lawlis's list doesn't account for the risks associated with taking ADD and ADHD medications for an extended period of time, including the possibility of serious reactions like psychosis and liver damage. In light of the fact that medication is only effective in about half of ADHD cases and that many kids are misdiagnosed in the first place, the risk medication may pose to your son's health may not be worth the potential reward.

I don't mean to say your son will necessarily experience any of these specific side effects if he takes medication. Neither am I advising you to simply ignore your doctor's advice. There are situations when medication truly is the best solution, and your child's may be one of them. What I am suggesting is, before you take that step, look at a doctor's ADD or ADHD diagnosis as one piece of the puzzle. Get a second opinion. Ask the doctor or psychiatrist to refer you to a therapist in your area who specializes in working with boys like yours to explore non-medical solutions. Consider enrolling your son in a well-regarded group program, where he can work through his issues and learn to find constructive outlets for his energy. I run one such program, called The Quest Project®, and have helped hundreds of boys overcome their challenges without the use of medication. I'll share more about that program later in the book.

Right now, understand that it's up to you to be your child's advocate, so be aware that there are options other than medication, and that one of them may be a better option for you and your son.

Sports

If there's one place where boys still generally get the type of support they need, it's on the court or the field in organized sports. Sports teach some of the vital lessons boys need to learn to become men: to work with their peers, to work toward and produce results, to handle the stress of competition, and what may be one of life's most important lessons—that sometimes they can control outcomes, and sometimes they can't. And since most sports teams are divided by gender, especially once kids reach their preteen years, boys get a chance to learn these lessons in a male-dominated environment. Coaches are frequently dads themselves, and they volunteer a considerable amount of time to help boys experience the fun, challenge, teamwork, and, yes, exercise that sports provide.

Good coaches model the kind of positive behavior from which boys benefit, and they provide boundaries, challenges, encouragement, and praise—all things boys need to mature into healthy, well-adjusted men. They teach boys what is and isn't appropriate in terms of risk-taking and aggression. They teach how to deal with the anger, disappointment, and other emotional issues that are part of playing the game.

But not every coach is a good coach, or even a good *man*. First, some coaches are women, especially as more women who were active in sports as girls become mothers and want to pass that experience on to their sons. More importantly, not all coaches are skilled at dealing with boys in a general sense, or at handling the different issues that come up in sports. Some coaches are not concerned with their players' success off the field, like their grades, social skills, or whether they're developing into good human beings. Some coaches care primarily about winning (and the bragging rights that come with it), and they may cross boundaries and break rules to maintain (or gain) an advantage. They may not pay much attention to what their players need, at least not beyond what they need to win. They may even directly contradict what parents want for their sons, if that conflicts with what's "best for the team."

But that's part of sports, and it's part of life. Overall, the support, life lessons, and opportunity to bond, test themselves, learn new skills, and have fun is usually more than worth any negative aspects. I personally credit sports with saving my life during my own difficult childhood. Sports gave me something positive to focus on and work toward when everything else in my life was in chaos. If your child is involved in sports, you can feel good that he's getting some extra support, as well as a bit of extra preparation for the ups and downs of the real world that boys who don't participate in athletics may be missing.

A Note for Fathers Who Coach

First of all, good for you. Your son gets to see you volunteer in the community and model good behavior in front of his peers. He also gets to spend time learning from you, rather than spend time learning from someone else's parent. These are all positive, healthy things, and you should feel good about them.

However, the time you spend coaching your son's team, as valuable as it is, should not be confused with those three to five hours you need to spend alone with him each week. As a coach, you're giving your time to *all* the boys, not just *your* boy. As a dad, you can, and should, give your son your undivided attention.

Religion

Many of us grew up with the guidelines, standards, and community provided by organized religion. But how instrumental were those institutions in teaching us what it means to be an adult? Church was a non-factor in my growing up—and I grew up in the Bible Belt!

In my experience working with boys, today's religious institutions don't play much of a role to guide them into manhood. Religion is less important in most people's everyday lives today than it was a few generations ago. According to statistics, the percentage of Americans who call themselves religious has been steadily dropping. Maybe it's different in your community. However, I still live and work in the heart of the Bible Belt, in St. Louis, Missouri, and maybe one of every ten boys who come into my office is involved in any religious activities.

For those boys who are involved in religion, the institutions and activities aren't providing much specific guidance to help them grow into good men. Coming-of-age rituals like Catholic Confirmation and the Jewish Bar Mitzvah focus more on ceremony than they do on teaching, testing, or challenging boys in a way that guides them into adulthood. Learning is generally focused on the memorization of facts, so the experience mimics what boys do in school and doesn't leave them feeling any more "grown up" when they're finished than they were when they began. Society reinforces this by failing to see or treat the boys any differently than they did before—because, frankly, they *are* no different.

Scouting and Service Organizations

Groups like the Boy Scouts provide a secular form similar to the coming-of-age experience in organized religion. Scouts earn badges and progress through ranks for volunteering in their communities, learning new skills, and accomplishing specific tasks, like tying knots and building fires. However, as of this writing, the Boy Scouts are no longer just for boys. The organization has given in to societal pressure and opened its doors to girls. This takes away another place where boys can spend time exclusively with male peers, exploring and learning about what it means to be a man.

Even before the Boy Scouts became the Boy and Girl Scouts (or maybe just the Scouts), the boys achieved most of their scouting accomplishments with the help of their parents, which often meant their mothers. And while weeding the vegetable beds at the community garden with Mom is a good and productive thing to do, it doesn't teach a boy much about what it means to be a man.

Ultimately, the badges boys earn are insignificant, because they're more about checking things off a list than they are about the transition to manhood. The boys don't change in any significant way to earn their badges. As with religious ceremonies, nothing happens that makes them *different*. So the larger society does not recognize the boys any differently.

Peer Pressures

In the absence of meaningful institutional support or any feeling of belonging to something bigger, most boys will look for validation from the one institution that's always there for them no matter what: their peers.

Having strong friendships with peers is important for boys' development and self-esteem. But what goes on within peer groups is not always constructive, and it does not always help boys learn what they need to know to be healthy, responsible men. Groups of boys tend to gather away from adult supervision, and the kid who is the most street-smart and experienced assumes the leadership position. He takes responsibility for teaching the other boys what he knows, "parenting" them in his own way. That could mean teaching them how to smoke a cigarette, how to steal a soda from a convenience store, or how to jump off the roof into the swimming pool—lessons that may be better left un-taught. And a boy who needs validation badly enough or is craving some sort of challenge in his life or wants nothing more than to prove himself and impress somebody can wind up in real trouble.

Maybe your son has been led down that path already.

If you experienced such a dynamic with your peers when you were growing up, you may be worried about it happening to your child. Or maybe you're starting to see signs of something in your son that makes you nervous. Maybe you worry he's heading down the wrong path, and you realize that you can't count on your son's school or any extracurricular institution like religion or scouting to provide him with the kind of guidance he needs to become the kind of man you want him to be.

Fortunately, when it comes to shaping your son's destiny and showing him what it means to be a man, you are a more powerful factor than all those other influencers combined. You just need to harness your power and use it to boost your son's growth.

CHAPTER 6

What Every Boy Needs to Become a Man

A dolescence, at its core, is the period during which a boy both physically and emotionally becomes a man. But what, specifically, does your son need from you to become the man he's supposed to be? What does it really take to be a Good Dad?

Obviously, the physical stuff will take care of itself. Your son will get taller, his voice will change, and he'll grow hair everywhere! A Good Dad is there to support his son through the emotional ups and downs of adolescence, some of which may be triggered by those physical changes.

Beyond the growing of hair and deepening of voice, at its most basic, fundamental level, the transition from boyhood to manhood is about a boy breaking away from his mother and learning to stand on his own two feet. This is not an easy transition for a child to make, and it's where you and your support are critical.

If your son is like most teenage boys, he probably feels confused. On one hand, he's being biologically drawn to this new world of men—enticed by the new challenges, new freedoms, and best of all, the chance to finally escape Mom's side and the constraints of being a "little kid" stuck doing little-kid things. On the other hand, all those big changes can be scary. Who can blame a twelve- or thirteen-year-old child for wanting to feel safe and cared for?

This is part of the reason teenage boys can be so difficult to deal with. One minute they're figuring out just how far they can push the boundaries; the next they want to run home and be reassured they're still loved and safe. They're fighting an internal battle they can't even begin to understand—and sometimes parents feel like their sanity is collateral damage. But your son doesn't need you to be his victim; he needs you to be his champion. He needs you to be *there*. Because with you by his side, he doesn't have to take those first scary steps toward manhood alone.

Good Dads help teenage boys navigate the emotional twists and turns of adolescence and understand that their uncomfortable feelings are normal—because Good Dads experienced them too. Good Dads let their sons know they're loved and accepted unconditionally, so they aren't afraid to try things and possibly fail. Good Dads provide the extra push a boy needs to feel the fear and do it anyway. And when a boy faces his fear and pushes past it, that's where real growth happens.

Unfortunately, it doesn't happen enough.

Why Some Boys Never Grow Up

Without that push from a father or other reliable male role model, too many boys get stuck. They don't get the support they need to succeed in the adult world, because there's no one around to teach them how to be in that world, or even how to make it to that world. As a result, many of them grow older without actually growing *up*.

This is another aspect of the systemic problem our society faces when it comes to boys becoming men. We see it everywhere—from dads screaming at each other on the Little League field to politicians calling each other names in the halls of Congress. America has become a nation of perpetual adolescents, men who have absolutely no idea how to behave in the adult world. The problem has been progressing for a few generations, but we're really seeing the extent of the damage today. At every level of society, our world is full of men who grew up without learning the skills adults need to have. They have lost pieces of themselves and of what it means to be a man. Our boys are just the latest casualty of this phenomenon.

Do you see the beginning of these effects in your son right now? Maybe he's having trouble in school, is abusing drugs or alcohol, or has been angry or aggressive. Or maybe he's simply acting distant and withdrawn. If he's like most of the boys I see in my practice, he may be depressed. He may even be suffering from PTSD.

Does Your Son Have PTSD?

Over the years, I've worked with dozens of boys who were on medication for ADD or ADHD who were, in fact, suffering from PTSD (post-traumatic stress disorder).

It may not seem possible for a child to suffer from a condition commonly associated with soldiers who have experienced the trauma of war. However, the National Center for PTSD defines PTSD as "a mental health problem that some people develop after experiencing or witnessing a life-threatening event, like combat, a natural disaster, a car accident, or sexual assault."

The concept of PTSD is confusing, because the condition causes many of the same symptoms that are commonly associated with Attention Deficit Disorders—symptoms that, according to the Mayo Clinic, "may include flashbacks, nightmares, and severe anxiety, as well as uncontrollable thoughts about the event."

I understand PTSD not only as a therapist, but also from personal experience. As a child, I was both a witness to and a victim of abuse, and I had no idea that the trauma I experienced at home was what made it difficult for me to pay attention in school. I didn't know it was the reason for what I later referred to as "intrusive thoughts" that made it impossible for me to concentrate on my studies. I didn't know it was at least partly responsible for my low grades. I just thought I wasn't as smart as the other kids.

If I were growing up today, I almost certainly would have been diagnosed with ADD or ADHD and put on medication. And that medication would not have helped me in any way, because my attention span was not my real problem. PTSD was.

While abuse triggered my PTSD, violence is not the only factor that can lead to this condition in a child. Everyday incidents like being bullied or rejected by peers can haunt kids into adulthood. Traumas like a death in the family or parents splitting up can also have long-term repercussions. Something we call "vicarious traumatization" happens when a child hears or sees the details of another person being abused or hurt. Kids can even get PTSD from something they see in a movie, on television, or in a violent video game. They play out the disturbing scene over and over again in their head as if it happened in real life.

This is why we advise parents to set boundaries around what they allow their kids to watch and play. When you say no to your son's request for that ultra-violent video game where the goal is to rip his opponent's head off, you're not being mean. It actually is for his own good.

It's important to understand that anything that causes stress, from TV zombies to parents fighting, can trigger intrusive thoughts in a child. Those thoughts can get in the way of a child's ability to concentrate and perform in school, and they can lead to other issues ranging from bedwetting to depression. If your son has difficulty concentrating or has anxiety or nightmares, take the next step and share your concerns with a professional therapist, preferably one with some experience in the area of PTSD. The sooner you get to the root of the problem, the sooner your son can begin to heal.

Whatever your son's specific issues are, whether or not you believe they're serious, it's important for you to take them seriously. Growing up doesn't magically heal the wounds of childhood. If your son doesn't get the help he needs while he's still a boy, he will most likely carry his issues into adulthood, where the pressures of life can make those wounds more painful and powerful. That's why it's crucial to step in now and provide your son with the support he needs.

The Power of Peers

Whether or not you take the time to offer your son the support he needs, he will find some sort of support somewhere. Boys are biologically hard-wired to seek out a male role model to help them through the transition to manhood. If you or some other reliable adult male doesn't step in with guidance, the easiest place for your son to find the mentor he craves is in his peer group. And that, as you might imagine, can be a recipe for trouble.

Think back to when you were a teenage boy. You probably had no idea what "manhood" meant. If you were like a lot of boys, you might have thought you proved you were a man by taking crazy risks like doing drugs or shoplifting or throwing rocks at cars to show everyone how brave you were. That kind of behavior is encouraged and rewarded within peer groups—just check out the book *Lord of the Flies* if you need a reminder of how powerful (and destructive) a group of teenage boys can be.

Since then, you've probably learned that becoming a man, at its core, means stepping up and accepting responsibility. Even if you're not quite there yourself, hopefully you're making progress in that direction. But when you were twelve or thirteen or even sixteen, you probably didn't know what real responsibility looked like or felt like.

Well, neither does your son.

The choice is simple: either you or some other responsible man takes the time to show your son what it means to be a man, or he'll learn someone else's version of what manhood means. That's why it's so important for you to step up now and begin guiding your son along the path to adulthood.

Five Things Boys Need to Transition to Manhood

A few generations ago, the transition between childhood and adulthood was almost automatic. Life was harder and shorter, and society needed kids to stop being a burden and start pulling their weight, so growing up was tied to the idea of accomplishment. Boys and girls learned to do specific tasks that contributed to the family and/or community, tackling bigger challenges as they got older and more capable. Growing into an adult meant being useful and productive, one step at a time, until a child was ready to take care of himself and others and pass on his wisdom to the next generation.

Today, our kids don't have the same kinds of challenges. The general consensus is that, because of this, they "have it easy." People call this generation of children "entitled" and accuse them of thinking they deserve more than they have. Our society places the blame for this squarely on the kids themselves. They fail to realize that, since there's no immediate need for kids to grow up, no one is stepping up to teach them how to do the things they need to do. And that's a tragedy. Children aren't born knowing how to accomplish tasks, interact with superiors, handle criticism, and get along with others. They need to be taught these things. And when we fail to teach our boys real-life skills or hold them accountable for their actions, we are setting them up to fail in the adult world.

However, if we provide the support they need to grow up healthy, happy, and responsible, if we teach them the things they need to know to be men, we give them a huge head start and make their time of transition much easier. Specifically, these five things are critical for a boy's transition into manhood:

1. Your boy needs a healthy male role model.

2. Your boy needs a safe "container" to deal with his pain.

3. Your boy needs the support of a community.

4. Your boy needs a sense of achievement, importance, and change.

5. Your boy needs a ritual to mark his transformation.

Let's look at each of these concepts in depth.

1. Your boy needs a healthy male role model.

If you're his father, that role model should be you. Your son's mother may work hard to give him what he needs, but only a man can show a boy what manhood means. That means you need to spend that three to five hours a week, every week, with your son providing guidance, answering his questions, and being present in his life so he knows that he matters to you. Playing *Call of Duty* together has its place, and ideally some of the quality time you spend with your son can be fun and relaxed, but your primary job is to provide boundaries and guidance. This is a crucial role, so if for some reason you are unable to fulfill it, make it a priority to find the right person to give your son the consistent, reliable, male support he needs. If you are that "other" person filling a father's traditional role, your presence may be even more important to that boy's development, so be sure to get the support *you* need to keep doing what you're doing. It's hard but very rewarding work.

2. Your boy needs a safe "container" to deal with his pain.

Emotional pain during adolescence is normal, even for boys who come from intact, functional families or boys who have a wide range of talents and skills and seem to have everything going for them. The confusion of breaking away from the safety of childhood and Mom can shake any boy to his core, no matter how smart or confident or "lucky" he appears to the outside world. Those "growing pains" can take on an extra dimension if a boy doesn't feel unconditionally loved and accepted by his father, like the majority of the boys I work with. And even if you think you're giving your son that love and acceptance, he may not be receiving it.

While you may not understand the source of your son's pain, it's important that you take it seriously. Some boys can manage the ups and downs of adolescence on their own, but yours may not be one of them. He may turn to coping mechanisms that will ultimately damage him, like drinking or using drugs, what mental health professionals refer to as "self-medicating." Abusing substances, or even sex, gambling, or food, to numb pain can set your boy up for a life of addictive behavior. Help him find a more constructive way to deal with his pain now. Even if your son doesn't act out, he may fall into a depression that can follow him into his adult years.

Understand that the pain of adolescence isn't something boys automatically outgrow—it can morph into behaviors and patterns that threaten success and happiness as an adult. Your job as his father and/or mentor is to help him experience and work through his pain by giving him a "safe space" to feel and process his feelings. It's important to withhold any judgment of what he is feeling or how he is coping. Instead, offer support by letting him know you understand he's having a hard time, that it's normal, that you trust him to get through it, and that, if he needs help dealing with his feelings, you are there for him. Don't try to fix the situation by saying *it will be okay* or *don't feel that way* or by trying to divert his attention. That sends the message that something is wrong when, in reality, things are probably completely normal. And if they're not, your support will give him the message that he can trust you enough to let you know.

"Growing pains" are one of the biggest challenges adolescent boys face. By offering your son the space and support he needs to deal with these feelings, you will help him move past them. This is one of the best ways to make sure your boy's childhood wounds don't follow him into his adult life.

3. Your boy needs the support of a community.

Just as men have migrated away from their small towns and farms since the Industrial Revolution, families have migrated away from the kind of tight-knit communities that used to offer boys a second, powerful level of support as they grew into men and took their place in society. In the past, helping boys transition to manhood was the responsibility of the community at large, partially because the community needed boys to grow up and pull their weight. So, teaching young men what they needed to know was considered an essential task.

These rituals still happen in other parts of the world, and even in some communities here in America. When a boy reaches a certain age, the male elders typically take the lead, taking the boy out of his home, away from his mother, and out into the wilderness. There, he is led through a series of challenges or tasks designed to teach him responsible behavior, prove his skills, give him a sense of accomplishment, and help him find his confidence and his identity as a man. This typically takes place over a period of days, and at the conclusion, there is usually a ceremony, often with a spiritual component. In that ceremony, the boy is welcomed by the elders into the world of men.

Today, churches, synagogues, Boy Scout troops, and other organizations offer a version of community complete with a guided passage to adulthood. As we explored previously, these rituals are long on ceremony and symbolism but short on the type of activities that actually teach boys things they need to know to be men or help them change in any meaningful way. So while the idea of a community of peers performing service together is good, and there's certainly nothing wrong with the experience, religious and service organizations alone aren't enough to provide boys with the type of community that will support them in this ultimate journey to manhood.

To give your son the kind of community support that will really benefit him—the support of a group of men—you probably need to make it happen by bringing other strong, responsible men into his life. Even if you're already spending three to five hours of quality time with your son every week, there are still things you don't know and can't teach him. He may have interests or skills that don't match up with yours, or he may simply benefit from other perspectives and experiences. Exposing him to men who can share wisdom you don't have will help your son discover more of his own talents and interests and develop them more fully.

Ultimately, the more healthy, responsible men your son knows and trusts, and the more these men take an interest in his development, the more supported he will be throughout his adolescence. He'll have more opportunities to connect with people he relates to who can help make a challenging time easier and more meaningful. Plus, by witnessing and participating in your son's transition to manhood, this community will be able to offer what Boy Scouts and churches cannot—validation of the adult your son is becoming. When these men tell him, "You did it. You're one of us now," the experience will be meaningful and profound—because it's *real*.

4. Your boy needs a sense of achievement, importance, and change.

It won't be enough for your son to know that you merely see he is changing. It's critical that you *recognize* and *celebrate* his accomplishments. Remember, the journey from boyhood to manhood is hard and sometimes painful. If your son makes progress toward becoming a man, and the most important man in his life doesn't even celebrate it, what's the point? Change means nothing if no one acknowledges it—especially if *you* don't acknowledge it for your son.

It's equally important, as your son progresses on this path, to avoid telling him what you *don't* want him to do or be. Obviously, you want to provide guidance and help him avoid making painful mistakes. However, these "don't be" messages that focus on your son's mistakes or failings don't really accomplish that goal. Instead, they send a message that, fundamentally, your son is doing something wrong, that he's not okay, that he doesn't measure up, and that he is not on the path to becoming the kind of man you will respect. This can set him up for a lifetime of depression.

When a boy thinks no one cares about him, that he will never amount to anything, or that he is worthless, he may reach the point where he believes nothing he does will matter. He may believe that he, as a human being, does not matter. This can lead to risky behavior, especially as he moves through adolescence where opportunities for risky behavior abound.

Instead of focusing on the things about your son that you think are wrong and need to change, keep your eyes open for those things your son is already doing *right*. Encourage those things, no matter how small they seem, and use them as a foundation to build from. Focusing on your son's talents, skills, and other good qualities will show him that you really *see* him. Knowing that he has the love and respect of his father will give him the message that what he does matters.

5. Your boy needs a ritual to mark his transformation.

You may not want to take your son into the wilderness and have him build a fire or kill a deer to prove he's a man. That doesn't mean he needs to become an adult without some acknowledgment that he's growing and changing and leaving behind the boy he was. Your son needs validation that he is different, that he is progressing on a worthy path, and that he is growing up. Ritual provides that validation.

A ritual doesn't need to be elaborate or formal. It can be as simple as taking some time away from the everyday routine to mark your son's transition. Take a walk or a bike ride, go out for ice cream or pizza, take him to see his first R-rated movie (if that fits with your value system). The details don't really matter. What matters is acknowledging to your son that you are doing this thing for a reason, that you know he is changing, that he's no longer a little boy, and that you recognize and are proud of the man he is becoming.

Knowing that his father can see his transformation into manhood is powerful validation for a boy. It also reminds him that you have his back—and that can be all a boy really needs to get through the hard times.

Give your son the support he needs, share in and celebrate his accomplishments, and you will enable him to become the man he's meant to be.

CHAPTER 7

Breaking the Cycle of Pain

F athers are vital to their sons' development. Ironically, they are usually the last family members I meet. Nine times out of ten (or more), it's the mom who drives a boy to my office, the mom who fills out the forms, and the mom who participates in the first session and answers background questions about the family. Dad usually doesn't show up until I ask for him.

When we meet for the first time, he's pretty sure he already knows what the problem is. It's that new kid his son's been hanging out with—he's trouble! Or maybe it's his son's mom—she's always been too soft on him, he needs to toughen up! Or it's the teacher who doesn't understand him, or the baseball coach who won't let him pitch, or it's just the fact that he's a teenager, and teenagers are supposed to be messed up, right?

Fathers almost never expect to hear that the real problem is *them*.

Then again, while they're almost always surprised by the news, underneath it all, they're not *that* surprised. You probably know on some level whether or not you've been doing all you can do or should do for your son (especially now that you know about the three to five hours a week of quality time you should be spending with him). You know the times that you've hurt him or felt ashamed or embarrassed about things you've done that have affected him or your family.

I want to assure you right now that I'm not here to give you a lecture and tell you you're a bad parent. Whatever has happened before this point in your son's life doesn't matter, because you're here right now. I'm not here to dwell on past mistakes. I'm here to advocate for your son, and if I'm going to advocate for him, I need to advocate for you too.

The Need for Healing

Dads who come to me for help with their sons wind up realizing their boys aren't the only ones who are hurting. I can't tell you how many fathers, during a discussion about adolescent development and what their son needs from them, say, "But no one did that for me!" Chances are no one did those things for you, either. Most of the dads I meet don't know how to teach their boys to be men for one very good reason: because no one ever taught them.

In fact, a lot of men are still struggling with the same issues that plagued them when they were teenagers. The kinds of problems your son is facing now don't usually go away on their own, and yours probably didn't either. Unless you've had some sort of therapy or dealt with your pain in a systematic way, your wound is still there, buried somewhere inside you, causing problems in your life, and maybe in your son's life too. Maybe you received your wound from your father, who was wounded from his father, who got it from his dad before him. It's a vicious cycle— but you have a chance to break that cycle now by working to heal yourself.

This is something I happen to know a lot about.

The Healing Process

You probably survived adolescence without having all five of the needs in the last chapter met. Most men do, and most of us think we turned out just fine—even if just barely. But while you probably don't realize it, missing out on that kind of vital support affected you growing up, and it may be affecting you today. And if your son isn't getting some, or all, of those kinds of support in his life, you can bet it's affecting him too.

My own childhood provides a pretty clear example of what happens to boys who don't get those five specific needs met. As the oldest child of an alcoholic father and a mother suffering from depression, my needs were not a priority. In fact, my parents relied on me to take care of my two younger siblings, so they didn't have to be bothered by our needs at all. I had to become a man without the most basic level of parental support, so it makes sense I missed out on a lot of the foundational stuff that's so important to a boy's development. Understanding how this shaped the man I became and learning how to heal from those wounds and become the man I was meant to be, formed the core of the work I do with boys and men today.

Let's take a closer look at what happens to a boy when those five decisive needs are not met.

1. If a boy lacks a healthy male in his life...

He will grow up without a role model to show him what being a man is all about. As an addict and an abuser, my dad was unable to fill that role for me. He made some effort at parenting when I was young—I remember him teaching me to tie my shoes when I was five—but that's one of the few pleasant memories of him that I have. As I got older and his alcoholism progressed, he became more like an abusive older brother than a dad. Occasionally, he would decide to teach me something new, but his teaching methods were more along the lines of throwing me in the deep end and expecting me to swim. He was too distracted to patiently show me, to let me try and fail, to point out what I did wrong, to let me try again, and to stick with me until I got it right. Looking back, I realize he thought he was teaching me to be tough, but he was only teaching me to fear. Instead of having a male role model to trust and model myself after, I learned that men were scary and caused pain.

Besides my dad, most of the men in my life were either impaired in some way or too busy to provide consistent support. But since I was a boy entering adolescence, I was biologically wired to search for male guidance wherever I could find it. I was lucky to find that guidance in sports. I had natural athletic talent, and even though my parents didn't care, my coaches did. They made sure I made it to practices and games when my parents couldn't be bothered to drive me. And since they gave me guidance and encouragement, they became the men I looked up to and tried to please.

After high school, I joined the military, which provided me with a whole hierarchy of male role models to look up to. It also provided me with an identity I could be proud of: I was no longer a boy, I was a military *man*. Unfortunately, that label alone wasn't enough to fill the hole where my father's love and support should have been. I grew up needy, seeking love and acceptance from everyone, especially women. I didn't have a clear idea of who I was or what mattered to me.

2. If a boy lacks a safe place (or container) to deal with his pain...

He will be unable to process those feelings in a healthy way. I could not talk to either of my parents about my pain, since they were the cause of so much of it. It's not like I could sit down with my dad and have a heart-to-heart talk about my hopes and dreams—he would have laughed in my face. Or worse, he may have *punched* me in the face. And my mom was too wrapped up in the abuse and her depression to worry about my problems. It wasn't just that I couldn't trust either of them enough to feel safe opening up to them. I knew they didn't care.

Instead of my home being a safe place where I could escape from the pressures of life, it was Ground Zero for those pressures. Home was where my parents would fight, where my dad would abuse me, and where I was responsible for making sure my younger siblings didn't make trouble, or else. Home was a place to run away from. Without a safe place to deal with my feelings, I pushed them down and tried to ignore them. As I got older, I learned to self-medicate, numbing my pain with alcohol and sex.

3. If a boy lacks the support of a community...

He will grow up feeling isolated and not understanding his place in the world. Community is where a boy learns the rules of society and how to do good things, and where he can be seen and get feedback. This steady presence, this "blessing of the community," helps a boy discover who he is and feel good about it. For a child, the first and most important community is the family. In my family, there were no rules to follow except "don't get caught," no one did anything good or even cared about what good was, and the only way to survive was *not* to be seen. I grew up feeling alone, without a sense of where I fit in or what I was supposed to do with myself. I lacked motivation and direction.

Ultimately, I found community in sports and, later, in the military. Both of these institutions gave me clear rules to follow, clear roles to step into, and clear goals to set for myself. They gave me a place to be seen doing well and to get feedback for my efforts. I don't know that I would have made it through adolescence and early adulthood without sports and the military. If my only community had been my peers, I may have ended up on drugs or in jail. Sports and the military gave my life structure and purpose until I started working on healing my wounds.

4. If a boy lacks a sense of achievement, importance, and change...

He will be slow to develop a sense of self. This wasn't a problem a few generations back, when boys became men working side-by-side with their dads. Their fathers were there to help them reach goals and make progress, so the transition to adulthood was all about gaining skills and self-esteem. Today, change is usually only evident through physical growth and the almost automatic progression through grades in school. Most dads aren't spending enough time with their boys to help them set goals and make choices that will guide them to manhood. Boys have to get there on their own.

The only goal my parents taught me was to get the hell out of their house. They lived in the moment, without thinking long term; thus, so did I. The only direction my father gave me was to tell me there were no more factory jobs and I wasn't smart enough to be a doctor, so I'd better figure out what I was going to do with my life. Sports gave me a sense of achievement. Later, the military did the same thing. But since I never developed a strong sense of self beyond those institutions, I depended on them to feel good about myself. When I unexpectedly lost my job in the military at the age of thirty, I had no idea who I was or what I was supposed to do. I was devastated.

5. If a boy doesn't experience a ritual to mark his transformation...

The things he accomplishes during his adolescence will be meaningless to him. Ritual is the culmination of these five crucial areas of support—it lets a boy know that everything he's gone through while growing up means something, which in turn gives his life meaning. The practice of rituals to celebrate and support boys has been lost over the past few generations. Back when a boy went out on the farm with his dad, he knew that someday, when he was ready, Dad would hand him the keys and say, "It's your turn to take over the tractor." Those rituals were built into life, so there were always milestones to celebrate.

Today, parents are too busy and stressed to take time out to celebrate much more than birthdays and holidays. My parents were completely disinterested in my accomplishments. They never came to any of my baseball or football games, so the one time my dad showed up to watch me compete—in the state pole-vaulting championship—I was so shocked to see him in the stands that I blew it. And of course, on the ride home, he took the opportunity to point out my failure. My parents weren't the type to say, "Good job!" when I succeeded, let alone say, "We love you just for being who you are," when I failed. So, I grew up starving for recognition, needing the approval of others to feel good about myself.

What did all of this mean in the long run? For me, lack of support in these five critical areas meant that, while I didn't know it, I was not emotionally ready for the demands of manhood. I did what I could to fill my needs myself, gravitating toward male-dominated institutions like sports and the military to give my life structure and purpose. I instinctively sought out male role models and male mentors. But while my military career flourished, the rest of my life was a mess. I married and divorced twice, and I was never in a relationship stable enough to have kids of my own. My successes were never enough to heal the wounds hidden inside me—I constantly needed a "fix" of some outside stimulant to keep me feeling good about myself.

I hope your childhood wasn't as bad as mine, although I've met people who have experienced far worse. The reason I share my story here is so you know you can trust me when I tell you that I know what boys and their fathers need. I want you to believe me when I say we, as men, have to do a better job, so your son can be the best man he can be.

CHAPTER 8

The Quest

I remember when I was a child, after surviving another day of yelling and screaming and abuse, lying in bed at night and talking to God.

I said, "I hope you're putting me through all of this hell for a reason."

It would take me more than thirty years—until I lost my job in the Air Force—to figure out what He had in mind.

Rock Bottom

The end of my military career sent me into a tailspin. I didn't just lose my job; I lost my support system, my identity, and my purpose in life. My ultimate goal of becoming a general was out of reach, and I had no idea what I was supposed to do with myself. I did the logical thing and went back to school for an advanced engineering degree, but I struggled with the same intrusive thoughts that made school almost impossible when I was a child. I felt like a failure.

I fell into a depression so deep that none of my usual crutches could pull me out—not booze, not women, not even booze *and* women. When my second marriage began to suffer, I realized I couldn't do it on my own. I signed up for couples' therapy.

I had never been to therapy before. As a military man, I had refused to even consider it, because I was afraid it would stigmatize me and hurt my career. Besides, in my mind therapy wasn't something Real Men did. Real Men didn't pay to lie on a stranger's couch and whine about their problems. Real Men toughed it out and kept that shit inside. But toughing it out wasn't working, and I didn't want to end up with a second divorce.

It turned out therapy was nothing like I expected. It wasn't awkward or embarrassing, it was freakin' awesome! For the first time in my life, someone cared enough to listen to me. When I told my therapist my childhood stories, she said "No wonder!" She told me that my problems weren't my fault, that I wasn't a bad person, and that I had a right to be happy and feel valued.

I finally felt heard. I felt validated. I wanted to go back every day.

A Path Emerges

After a while, I realized I didn't want to go back to therapy just because it made me feel good. I was also interested in the way therapy worked. I wanted to understand how my therapist was helping me heal from the wounds of my childhood. How did she know what to say and how to advise me—and could I help people the same way? I switched my major from engineering to psychology and started researching the field, reading everything I could get my hands on, talking to my therapist about her work, even visiting the state mental hospital. Eventually, it became clear that while my marriage could not be saved, I could. I had found a new purpose in life.

But after a year or two, I felt stuck. I understood my problems better, I had gotten over my depression and found my direction, but I wasn't making progress beyond that. I didn't realize it at the time, but by giving me the nurturing my mother had failed to provide, my therapist had helped me recover from what I missed during the first half of my childhood. I was ready to move on and find a male role model to help me deal with the damage done by my dad.

My next therapist, a male, became that role model. Unlike my first female therapist, who spent most of her energy telling me I was okay, this new therapist challenged me to take an active role in my healing. He gave me homework and demanded accountability, pushing me to set goals for myself and figure out how to get there. He also gave me my first exposure to group therapy. Every Thursday night, I would meet with a group of men for three hours and hash out all kinds of problems, sometimes using visualization and other "experiential" techniques. I soaked it all up. After all, I wasn't just healing; I was also learning.

Between my studies and my therapy, I started to see patterns. I noticed that through generations of thinkers, from Plato and Socrates to Freud and Jung, psychology continued to address the same basic problems—problems that were usually rooted in childhood. I also studied the work of child development experts like Erik Erikson, and I started to put together the pieces of the puzzle, beginning with my own issues. I figured out what I missed as a child, and how the absence of both of my parents, especially my father, shaped the person I became.

The Vision

My "aha" moment came when, at my therapist's suggestion, I signed up for a "Vision Quest." He was one of the counselors on staff at an all-male wilderness weekend designed to help men deal with their issues in an intensive, experiential setting. A few days later, I was alone in the wilderness, pondering my life up until that point and the mistakes I'd made. I tried to understand my purpose in the world, and how it all fit together.

Why was I put on this planet? What am I here to do?

I didn't really know. But a Vision Quest is designed to spark a "vision" that can provide guidance for the journey ahead. That's the whole point of the experience—to give you a sense of what you're on this planet to accomplish and show you where to go next. And when my vision came, it did not disappoint:

I am seeing the world from the moon. I see a gray mass moving toward me from the top of the earth, coming over the North Pole. I look closer and realize that the gray mass consists entirely of boys, and they are all headed to me for help.

I am the light they are moving towards—they want to escape the dark.

It may have been a little "out there," but to me it made perfect sense. The pain I had experienced in my life, that brought me to therapy and ultimately to this Vision Quest, wasn't just about me. The world was full of boys who were suffering just like I had suffered, who were being abandoned physically or emotionally by their fathers, and who were at risk of growing up to carry that pain into adulthood, just like I did. As a psychology student planning a career in therapy, I was in a unique position to do something to help those boys.

Turned out God had a reason for putting me through hell, after all.

The Foundation

Before I could help anyone else, I needed to finish my work on myself. That included not only getting emotionally healthy, but also finishing my degree. I decided to concentrate on developing a way to help boys heal, and I used myself and my own healing process as a case study. As I figured out what specific things I missed growing up and how they affected me, I then researched and conducted experiments to develop ways to fill those empty places for me and to apply that same process to help boys heal from similar experiences.

Thus, The Quest Project® was born.

I supplemented my healing and education with as much field experience as I could find, including working as a case manager at the Judevine Center for Autism. To learn more about how other people dealt with pain, I joined the staff on other Vision Quest weekends. To get experience with adolescent boys, I volunteered as a Big Brother for five different kids, and I volunteered at an organization called the Pride Program, dedicated to helping gang members find alternatives to life on the streets. Eventually, as I progressed through my psychology studies, the program's leader, Henry Thurman, invited me to co-lead with him, and we started implementing some of my suggestions. This gave me a glimpse of how my own vision might someday come to life.

The Experiment

Once I graduated and earned my credentials, I had to establish myself as a therapist and build experience and a reputation for working with boys. At first, I worked with patients one-on-one, and I took a part-time therapist position at a local clinic to gain experience and exposure. After being there for some time and getting to know the decision makers, I convinced the hospital directors to let me start a boys' group.

I recruited a group of five boys to work with me once a week, and I created a program based on the psychological theories I had studied and the research I had done in school and through my own healing process. I had an idea of where I wanted things to go based on my own experiences—I wanted to provide the boys with those five urgent things they needed to become healthy men:

1. A healthy male role model (me)

2. A safe container (confidentiality)

3. A sense of community (the people in the group)

4. A sense of achievement, importance, and change (progress made in group)

5. A celebration ritual (validation and something to mark the transformation)

However, since I'd never run a group on my own and didn't know exactly what to expect, I made a conscious decision to keep the process fluid, so I could change things up as I went along. I had never created an entire program for anyone other than myself, and I knew I needed to be free to shape the experience according to how the boys progressed and what they needed next.

It was a bit of a seat-of-my-pants operation—I wasn't sure what would happen or how the boys would react. However, within a few weeks, it became clear that what I was doing was working. The boys were feeling better, and their attitudes were changing. The parents were excited about their sons' progress. I realized that I had created something that could make a real difference.

When I finished with my second group of boys at the hospital, I knew I was ready. I officially launched The Quest Project®.

The First Quest®

I still have the spiral notebook where I put the very first program together. I sketched out a ten-week journey designed to take a group of boys through a modern-day rite of passage, taking my inspiration from the initiation rituals in ancient and native cultures, as well as my own Vision Quest experiences. I knew I would serve as a role model and create the rules that would provide a safe container where the boys could do their work. The community element would come in the form of a group of boys working together and supporting each other. The program included weekly challenges to give the boys a sense of achievement and change and a graduation ritual at the end to celebrate their accomplishment.

I designed every element of the program with a specific therapeutic purpose—guiding the boys through the process of first uncovering their pain, then facing it, and finally healing from it as they progressed from week to week. At the same time, it helped them discover the men they wanted to be, set meaningful goals, and lay a strong foundation toward achieving them.

Soon, I had eight troubled boys, ranging from sixteen to eighteen years old, ready to put Quest®—and me—to the test.

I saw results in less than a month.

By the third week, those eight boys were so different that parents were calling me to ask, "What is going on with my son?" Week by week, the boys grew closer as a group, helping each other through the exercises, holding each other accountable, and soaking up the lessons and experiences I had designed. But the real difference came in their everyday lives, as they applied at home and at school the new tools and strategies they learned in Quest®. The transformations were dramatic. One boy who was a chronic pot smoker quit and pledged to stay clean. Another boy who refused to talk to his mother found a way to communicate with her again.

Parents kept calling to thank me, but I was the one who was grateful. Those boys and their parents showed me that my research and all the hands-on work I had done—not to mention my own painful childhood—had paid off. They were proof that I had developed a way to help boys heal.

The Quest Project® worked.

The Evolution

Since that first session eighteen years ago, I've made a lot of changes to the program. I've added more parent sessions, since parents continually asked for more involvement and advice, and having an involved parent really boosts the odds of a child's success. I've cut the number of boys in each session to five, to give each boy more time and attention and to take some of the pressure off myself (working with ten boys was exhausting!). I made other changes and tweaks to the program as I noticed where the boys were getting stuck and what additional help they needed to move forward.

More recently, I've taken The Quest Project® on the road, so that boys outside the St. Louis area where I'm based can benefit from the experience. I've conducted several weekend sessions where the steps are condensed into two days of intensive activity. I'm training other therapists to deliver The Quest Project® to boys in their areas. And in the midst of writing this book, I launched the first-ever Quest Project® with a group of adult men, taking them through the same healing process many of their sons had experienced. You'll meet some of them later in this book.

Overall, however, the basic structure of The Quest Project® has remained the same as that first program I sketched out in that spiral notebook back in the year 2000. With the exception of those weekend sessions, I still take boys through a ten-week modern-day rite of passage designed to help them uncover and confront their pain, discover what they care about, and meet the men they are meant to be. I've worked with over two thousand boys in the past twenty-five years, all of whom are making their mark in the world in their own way. One works for the space program at NASA. One is a hockey player in the NHL system. One boy, who told me he wanted to be a serial killer, is now a lawyer. One is a dentist. Many are firemen, and many more are serving their country in the military, just as I once did. Some of them have even decided to become therapists or counselors.

They're all paying it forward in their own way, just like I've been able to. And that makes me extremely proud.

I've committed my life to fostering this kind of change with the boys I work with and their fathers. Now I want to help you and your son.

CHAPTER 9

The Quest Project®—An Overview

B y this point, you may be wondering exactly what happens during the ten weeks of The Quest Project® and how it prepares adolescent boys for adulthood. In this chapter, I'll share a basic overview of how the program progresses, the issues we deal with, and how we address them to help boys heal their pain, move beyond their self-destructive behaviors, and discover the men they're meant to become.

While having a trained facilitator like me, as well as the support of the group of boys, is a key element of the program, there may not be a Quest Project® available in your area (although my team and I are working on that). I've included the following pages to give you an idea of the progression I use in the program, along with some ideas that can help you and that can help you and your son face and work through his—and your—challenges.

Please be advised that, as an experienced, licensed therapist, I understand how to work with the intense emotions a process like The Quest Project® might trigger, and because I am an outsider, it is much easier for me to be objective than it is for a parent who loves and worries about his son. So, to help you apply some of The Quest Project® techniques with your own child and get the most out of this book, I conclude each step in the program with special tips and modifications designed especially for fathers or mentors who want to work with their boys and/ or on their own healing.

Here are some things to remember before we begin:

1. While I've tried to give you an overview of the challenges adolescent boys face in this book, there is much more to learn. Do some additional reading about how boys develop and what they need. Consider working with a counselor to help you set goals, prepare for what's to come, and formulate a plan to organize, schedule, and work with your son.

2. Form a group with other dads for support and feedback as you go through the process. Your son might not need this, but chances are you will, especially if you decide to use this process to heal your own wounds.

3. Set a schedule and get feedback from your son about your plans before you start. For best results, your son should feel like a willing participant in whatever work you do, and not like it's being forced on him. However, you're the parent, and what happens is ultimately up to you.

4. Buy a punching bag (I'll explain this later).

5. Keep it simple, especially when you discuss feelings with your son—remember his attention span! I limit my discussions of feelings to what I call "The Big Four": Mad, Sad, Glad, and Afraid.

6. Start each "session" with your son by offering a treat you know he likes—pizza and soda, ice cream, etc. The treat doesn't have to be food-related, just a way to establish that your time together is special and positive before you get down to business.

7. Establish the ground rules and natural consequences before you start.

Remember, you'll be doing a deep dive into some difficult emotional territory, for you and for your son, so try to keep things positive and remain in control of your emotions throughout the process. Also remember that change doesn't happen overnight. Try to minimize expectations and allow yourself to go with the flow. If you find yourself or your son struggling with any of these exercises, or if they unearth feelings or behaviors you don't feel comfortable dealing with on your own, get some professional help.

The Basics

The Quest Project® consists of ten group sessions, usually one per week, each lasting ninety minutes. The overall program is specifically designed to provide the five decisive things a boy needs to become a man:

1. A healthy male role model

2. A safe "container" to deal with his pain

3. The support of a community

4. A sense of achievement, importance, and change

5. A ritual to mark his transformation

There are five parent meetings during the ten-week session: one at the beginning, one at the end, and three at pivotal points in the middle of the program, when I've discovered that parents need the most support to handle the changes their sons are experiencing.

When I run groups, I separate the boys by age. I've found groups of boys aged eleven to thirteen, fourteen to sixteen, and seventeen to nineteen work best. This ensures that the boys who take this journey together form a supportive community; since the boys are around the same stage of their development, they can relate to each other as peers and feel comfortable, not intimidated, sharing their experiences. I also limit the size of each group to just five boys, so each child gets the individual time and attention he needs to get the most out of the experience.

The ten-week program follows this path:

Week 1 – Container Building

When the boys come to their first meeting, they usually don't know me very well, and they are total strangers to each other. So, our first session is dedicated to establishing the trust the boys need—in me and in each other—to do the work we're about to do. I always kick it off the same way, with the same question:

How the HELL are you doing tonight?

You might be wondering why a mental health professional would choose to begin an intensive, deeply personal treatment program with a (mild, but still offensive to some) four-letter word.

It's all about establishing trust.

The boys I work with have never been in a program like The Quest Project® before, and they have no idea what to expect. Many of them walk in feeling fearful and uncertain about what might happen to them. By stepping down off my pedestal immediately and revealing myself as an approachable, real, normal human being—who uses four-letter words and everything!—I let them know that I'm not so different from them. Right off the bat, they see that I'm not a parent or a teacher or a coach who's going to judge them, correct them, or shame them. I'm not going to tell them who or how to be. I'm there for one reason and one reason only: to make their lives better.

I call this first meeting "Container Building," because our first task together is to establish a safe space where boys (or men, depending on the group) can feel free to be fully and completely themselves and share things that are deeply personal. Most of the kids I see have never talked with anyone else about the kinds of issues we will explore. So, we establish ground rules to make sure everyone feels as comfortable as they possibly can when talking about uncomfortable subjects. The boys are free to express themselves however they want to, and we pledge to each other that whatever is said in our meetings will remain confidential. That means they know I won't go back to their parents and "rat them out."

That said, I am legally and professionally obligated to make some exceptions to this rule. If a boy demonstrates what is called suicidal or homicidal ideation (an intention to harm himself or someone else), or if he has been abused, I am mandated to report those cases. But those cases are rare.

After the ground rules have been established, we go around the room and have each boy introduce himself. I ask him to tell the group two things:

1. Why he thinks he's in the program; and

2. Why his parents say he's in the program.

As you might expect, those are often two completely different stories.

But at the same time, the boys' stories are often similar to each other, which helps them see that they are not so different and that their problems are not unique. It's the first step in building a supportive community where the boys can get down to the business of uncovering and dealing with their issues and changing their lives.

Try This at Home...

If you plan to guide your son through this process, I highly recommend beginning with at least three sessions (for you, not your son) with a reputable counselor or therapist. Tell the therapist what you're planning to do, and ask them to help you state your intent (what you plan to do) and build your "container" (establishing ground rules and a schedule to follow).

Once you're ready to get things started with your son, here's an exercise to get the ball rolling:

Meet Your Fantasy Dad!

This exercise is a (brief, adolescent-boy-friendly) version of the Fantasy Son exercise at the beginning of the book. This time, it's your son's turn to write down everything he wishes he had in a dad, while you write down the characteristics of your own version of what your perfect father would have been like. Then share your fantasy fathers with each other. You should probably plan to go first (unless your son wants to start) and model the process for him.

Remember, for this and every exercise, there are two cardinal rules:

NO judging! Judging destroys the trust you're trying to build.

Keep it brief! Always keep your son's attention span in mind.

Week 2 – Goal Setting

Most teenage boys don't have clear goals for the coming month, let alone the rest of their lives. However, if your intention is to get somewhere, you need to know where that somewhere is, otherwise you'll just wander around aimlessly. So, we dedicate our second session to Goal Setting, which gives the boys a clear picture of what they will be working toward during their time in The Quest Project®.

Setting goals together as a group gives the boys two things everyone needs to reach a goal: support and accountability. However, since most boys have never actually set and worked toward this type of long-term goal, we set our goals in a way that's probably different from any goal-setting they may have done in school. Boys learn visually and through experience (as opposed to just listening), so I take them through a guided imagery exercise that helps them discover the men they want to be. The exercise also helps them identify and name the things that are standing between them and their goals, so each boy has a clear picture of what he will be working to overcome in the remaining weeks of the program—and afterwards.

This exercise helps the boys establish a direction and a purpose for their journey, and it clarifies that wherever they are in that moment, they are beginning a process that will take them to a better place.

Try This at Home...

Visualization is something anyone can do relatively easily—even you. So for this week's exercise, visualize the man (and the father) you want to be, as well as whatever obstacles are standing in your way. Then ask your son to do the same thing. When you're finished, share what you visualized, keeping in mind those cardinal rules:

1. NO judging!

2. Keep it brief!

The goal is to help your son think differently about his life and the challenges he faces.

Week 3 – The Tool Box

As we explored earlier in this book, all adolescent boys experience pain of one kind or another. Their pain is almost always responsible for any problem behavior or emotional issues. This week's exercise is designed to help boys recognize, understand, and deal with the wounds that are causing their pain. Because it can be a rough week, I hold a parents' meeting in advance of the session, to help them prepare for the emotions their sons will be dealing with and to be ready with an appropriate response.

This exercise introduces the boys to their metaphorical "Tool Box." This box is filled with all the negative and positive unconscious messages they've internalized throughout their lives. Part of this exercise is dedicated to figuring out exactly where these messages came from. In a lot of cases, the blame falls squarely on Mom and Dad. This awareness leads many boys to conclude that, "My parents have given me a bunch of shit!"

Don't worry, this exercise is not designed to make your child hate you. In therapy we say, "You have to go through the crap to heal the crap." But first, you have to actually *identify* the crap. When the boys understand that they were not, in fact, born with their crap and that someone else (maybe you) put the crap there by criticizing them or judging them, they feel empowered to give that crap back to the responsible party.

(Now you understand why I hold a parent meeting before this session.)

However, I don't send the boys home covered (just to extend this metaphor as far as it can possibly go) in crap. After we help them uncover the negative messages that have caused them pain, we end the exercise by looking for the positive messages that are also hidden in their Tool Boxes. These include any messages from their parents that they are wanted and loved. That way, we send the boys home on a high note.

Still, it's important to know that this may be a difficult week. In many cases, it's the first time a boy will be forced to look at the painful feelings and emotions he has been suppressing. When the boys go home afterwards, with a whole week before the next session, it's not uncommon for them to act out physically, verbally, or both.

Enter the punching bag.

In my professional opinion, a punching bag is a must-have tool for anyone raising an adolescent boy. They are built for one purpose and one purpose only—to take a punch, or several punches. The punching bag is a safe and effective vehicle for boys to release their anger, as opposed to punching their walls, their doors, or their siblings.

Try This at Home...

Asking your son to uncover the negative emotions he's been storing inside can be scary and difficult. If you've been working with a counselor, schedule a session in advance, walk them through what you're planning to do, and get some coaching on how to facilitate the exercise and deal with the aftermath. When you do guide your son through uncovering his stored negative messages, model the process by doing the exercise with him. Go first and share some of the negative messages you uncover about yourself, so he knows he's not alone and that you're playing on a level field. Share plenty of your own positive messages and encourage him to find his as well.

Week 4 – Clean Up

Week 3 leaves a lot of emotional debris to deal with—which is why Week 4 is all about finishing what we've started. In Week 4, we focus on pain, diving even deeper to find hidden wounds that the boys may not be aware of. Identifying these last, most deeply buried wounds prepares a boy to wipe the slate clean and begin the healing process.

The exercise we use to accomplish this starts with each boy drawing an outline of his own body. Inside the outline, I have them draw and label physical and emotional wounds that didn't come to them as messages, but as a result of pivotal events in their lives.

I ask all the boys to start by drawing a broken heart, to represent the pain that brought them to counseling in the first place. But after that, they're free to draw and label any wound they remember—from physical wounds like falling off a bike and breaking an arm, to illnesses like tonsillitis or chicken pox, to more traumatic events like being beaten up by a bully or hit by a parent.

This exercise uncovers extremely traumatic experiences, such as abuse, which makes it a potentially difficult and emotional week for the boys. However, it's all in service to help them get to the bottom of their wounds. Once they hit bottom, they can begin the process of building themselves back up.

Try This at Home...

While this exercise can be intense and emotional, it is still okay to do it at home, with a few modifications. First of all, DO NOT attempt to deal with serious issues like abuse on your own. You will need to work with a professional to help guide your son through recovery from that type of experience. Second, as with all of the exercises we've done so far, start by drawing your own map and pointing out your own wounds. This shows your son how it's done and that you have his back.

For your son's map, ask him to stick to smaller wounds, like a fight with a friend, feeling shamed at school, or being yelled at by his family. This will keep your son moving forward through the process, and it will give you a chance to learn more about the types of issues he's dealing with. If any of your son's issues feel "too big" for you, like abuse or PTSD, enlist the help of a professional therapist or counselor.

Week 5 – The Anger Shadow

Anger gets a bad rap. Sure, it can make people lose control and drive them to do stupid, destructive, and even dangerous things. But anger is also a completely normal and even necessary emotion.

Your son's anger may be the primary reason you seek help for him right now. It's a major reason most parents bring their boys to The Quest Project® in the first place. However, while anger is common, and problems with anger are almost equally common, Week 5 teaches boys that their anger isn't the real problem. The problem is how they deal with it.

To get the ball rolling, I start the session by talking about my own history with anger, showing where I broke my hand in a fight and talking about the anger-related messes I made in my life, both as a teenager and as an adult. I then explain how I identified what I call my "Anger Shadow," which is the thing I did to express my anger. Finally, I (briefly) explain how I learned to change that behavior and change my life for the better.

Once I've shared my story, each boy gets a chance to talk about his own "Anger Shadow" and the trouble that behavior has caused in his life. Their answers vary. "When I get angry, I punch the wall." "When I get angry, I drink alcohol or smoke pot." "When I get angry, I burn my arm with a cigarette." I ask them to specifically identify three things they do when they get angry at home, and three things they do when they get angry at school, since different environments usually provoke different results.

Then comes the healing. I ask each boy to choose a new behavior to substitute for the Anger Shadow the next time he gets angry, and to state to the group what he plans to do. Through this process, the boys learn that their *actions* are the problem, not their *feelings,* and that as long as they control and are accountable for their actions, they don't need to feel bad or guilty about their completely normal feelings of anger.

Try This at Home...

After two tough weeks, this one should feel a little easier—and as usual, it starts with you. Own up to your own anger, including times you've gotten angry at your son, and the things you've done in anger that you now regret. This will help your son understand that not only is his anger normal, his "Anger Shadow" is normal, too. Encourage your son to share his own stories of times he was angry and the ways he reacted.

Next, tell him what you plan to do to handle your anger more constructively in the future. Make a commitment to react differently, just as the boys do in The Quest

Project® session and ask your son to help you brainstorm more constructive ways for both of you to deal with your anger.

And don't forget that punching bag!

Week 6 – Anger Work

Week 6 consistently ranks as a highlight of The Quest Project®—a week when all of our work leading up to that point starts to pay off in a big, dramatic way. The exercise, called "Anger Work," is designed as an elaborate initiation ritual, complete with incense and drums, that helps the boys release their anger in the most cathartic and complete way possible.

When the night begins, I tell the boys that their lives are about to change forever, that they will shed their boy skin, and that the man inside them will emerge. Next, I go around the room and ask each boy to visualize and identify his anger, and to bring it to the surface. Once that anger has been identified, I hand the boy a baseball bat and tell him to let loose on the punching bag—for as long as he needs or wants to.

The reactions are emotional and intense. Some boys will whale on the bag for ten or twenty minutes until they're totally exhausted. Some boys throw up. Some cry, because often, the emotion behind their anger is sadness.

Once each boy has had his turn on the punching bag, I have them stand up as a group. I tell them that a change has taken place—they are no longer little boys, they are young men.

Finally, with all that anger gone, I tell the boys to choose what they want to take in to replace the anger that they have expelled. With a gentle hint from me, they choose joy. Each boy gets to identify what joy means to him, and as a young man, he accepts the responsibility for providing it. This begins to lift the lid off of the boys' depression and open them up to the possibilities their lives hold.

Try This at Home…

Now is the time to take out the punching bag (if you haven't already). I do not advocate using a bat at home; fists will do just fine here. Take turns (you start) talking about what makes you angry (hint: don't start with your son or your spouse; try more neutral or even funny things like your boss, politics, traffic, whatever), and give the bag a whack. Don't forget to switch off, and no matter how cathartic it might feel, remember that this is about your son. Be sure he gets as much time as he needs to punch the bleep out of whatever makes him angry. If you keep it light on your end, this exercise can be a lot of fun and a great bonding experience. And chances are you'll both get a great night's sleep afterwards!

Week 7 – Conflict Resolution

The boys typically experience a dramatic change at this point in the program. After the "initiation" they experienced the previous week, they are more bonded as a group, and they walk taller and prouder as individuals. Now that the boys are officially "young men," it's time for them to begin to master some adult skills. Specifically, adults are expected to take responsibility for things that upset them and work toward resolving them. That's why Week 7 is dedicated to Conflict Resolution—it's all about teaching boys a more satisfying and effective way to deal with the things that bother them.

We start with each boy identifying a conflict with someone—usually a parent. Then we use the conflict resolution tool to work through a process that ensures both sides are heard and a deeper understanding can be reached. The tool takes each participant in the conflict through a series of steps, while the other participant listens. The listener then repeats back what the first person said, to ensure that they heard it correctly.

When the exercise is finished, each person better knows and understands how the other person feels. Understanding goes a long way toward resolving conflict.

This process helps boys understand that there are always two sides to a conflict, and that when both of those sides are presented and discussed calmly, a resolution can often (not always, but often) be reached. The exercise is designed for the boys and their parents to do at home, and I teach it to the parents, too.

We then do a second exercise that I call Dad/Not Dad. It dramatizes the choice most boys believe they are facing: "Will I grow up to be like my dad, or NOT like my dad?" Boys with Absent Fathers have an especially hard time choosing between *emulating* a person who has hurt and disappointed them and trying to *eliminate* any trace of their father in their personality.

We employ a visualization exercise that helps boys discover a third way. Instead of having to choose between being "Dad" or "Not Dad," they can choose to be someone much better—themselves. The exercise gives them the freedom to emulate their fathers in the areas they admire without feeling destined or doomed to make the mistakes they feel their fathers have made. They learn the difference between being their father and being their father's son. For a lot of the boys, this is the first time they realize that they have this choice. Learning they can be exactly who they want to be, and that they are not doomed to either repeat their father's mistakes or reject him entirely, is empowering.

Try This at Home...

The Conflict Resolution exercise is designed to be done with your son, so go to TheQuest-Project.com to download the worksheet. You may want to enlist a mediator the first time you try the exercise to keep both you and your son on task and make the experi-

ence more enjoyable. If you elect to do it alone, remember to listen and not to judge or get angry or offended. Let your son "be heard."

The Dad/Not Dad exercise can be highly emotionally charged, especially if you ARE Dad, and the exercise invites your son to reject aspects of who you are. If you're convinced you can keep your own feelings out of it and you'd still like to try it, I recommend working with a mental health professional who can help guide you and your son through the process.

Week 8 – The Gift

In the fairy tale *Iron Hans*, a boy embarks on a mythical Hero's Journey to find his lost "Gift," which, in the story, is a golden ball. In our Week 8 session, the boys are guided through a visualization that takes them on their own personal Hero's Journey to find their own unique Gift.

I start by asking the boys to visualize losing their Gift for a very specific reason— because their parents haven't acknowledged it and made it feel real. I'm not doing this to make the parents' lives difficult. But the fact is that failing to see or value a child's Gift is something parents tend to do unconsciously. So, I encourage the boys to feel anger and sadness at the loss.

From this starting point, I guide the boys through a visualization that takes them through each step of their Hero's Journey on a quest to recover their Gift. The boys grow at each stage of the journey, and at the end, each boy recognizes that his Gift is actually a part of him—the quality that he thinks of as the most special and powerful thing about him. Then, one by one, the boys step up and name their Gifts. Typically, I hear things like, "My gift is my athletic ability;" "My gift is my intelligence;" or even, "My gift is my heart."

The point of the exercise is to help each boy identify his true strength, as opposed to those things he has been told he's good at. There's usually a big difference between the two, and helping a boy express and claim what he knows makes him special teaches him to articulate not only that he is unique and talented, but exactly how and why. That makes it real.

Try This at Home...

Get the ball rolling by talking about what you know your Gifts are and how you use them in the world. Then encourage your son to do the same thing. Remember not to question, judge, or suggest what you think his Gifts are. Give him the freedom to express what he knows is true about himself, as opposed to what you see in him.

Week 9 – Relationships and Forgiveness

Once we've dealt with the pain and anger of our boys, and we've given them some tools to both visualize and help bring about a better future, it's time to deal with something that inevitably will be in every boy's future—relationships. Teenage years mark our first experiences with love. However, boys with Absent Fathers grow up lacking a strong male perspective on relationships, from basic sex education to an understanding of how healthy relationships work. Week 9 of The Quest Project® is dedicated to exploring the subject of relationships.

In Week 9, we talk about what love means, the difference between "love" and "in love," and even a little bit about sex (as is age-appropriate for the group). We also address the topic of forgiveness, because in any relationship between two human beings, there are bound to be misunderstandings and even betrayals. The concept of forgiveness is essential to maintaining a healthy relationship.

The boys use the same conflict resolution tool we introduced in Week 7 to work through the process of forgiving someone who has hurt or wronged them. We start by asking the boys who they need to forgive in their lives, and they usually don't have a problem coming up with someone. In many cases, that person is Mom or Dad. They then use the tool to work toward forgiving that specific person.

The hidden bonus to this forgiveness work is that, while they work through the reasons to forgive someone else, they learn something even more valuable—how to forgive themselves.

Try This at Home…

Before you attempt this new version of the conflict resolution process, take some time to define what "love" and "in love" mean to you. Read up on the topics of love and forgiveness and think about the people in your life who you need to forgive. It's important to process your own feelings before you work with your son, so you can be fully focused on him.

When you're ready, work through the conflict resolution exercise from Week 7 with a new focus on forgiveness. Model the process for your son by talking through your own process of forgiving someone who wronged you. Then invite your son to do the same. Remember, no judging, especially if it's about you!

Week 10 – Purpose = Mission

By the final week of The Quest Project®, the boys have gained a wide range of skills—from healthier ways to process anger to effective tools for conflict resolution and forgiveness. They've worked through their pain and discovered their gifts. They're ready to step into their roles as adult men, which means it's time for them to decide who and what they want to be.

That happens in our final exercise, Purpose = Mission. This exercise helps the boys take stock of their newfound skills and choose how they want to use them in the world. It helps them decide on the path to follow as they grow into healthy, happy young men who are ready to contribute something to society and use their unique gifts to make a difference. As an example, I tell the boys my own mission: "To create healthy lifestyles by teaching, facilitating, writing, research, and example." Figuring out how and where they want to use their gifts is an exciting way to end this chapter of their lives and move into the next one.

Try This at Home...

This final experience should be an enjoyable experience for both you and your son, as it's an opportunity to focus on goals and dreams and how to make them come true. If you already have an idea of what your personal mission is, you've got a head start. If not, identify what you want to accomplish with your life, and then share that mission with your son. Model the progression of steps to achieve a goal by telling him what steps you have taken or will take to make your mission a reality.

Next, help your son share his vision of his life's mission, and then work with him to create a step-by-step action plan to turn his goal into reality. Remember, this is about what he wants, not what you want, and your job is to support the vision for his future that excites him. If he says, "I want to be President of the United States," or "I'm going to play shortstop for the Yankees," your job is not to tell him why that's unrealistic, but to help him work out the very real steps he would need to take to achieve his goal.

Graduation

As I mentioned earlier in this book, an adolescent's transformation from boy to man doesn't feel real unless and until it is recognized and celebrated by his community. That's why we end each ten-week session or weekend intensive of The Quest Project® with a full-blown graduation ceremony, where each boy takes his turn standing before his parents, his peers, and the entire group to say, "This is who I am now."

In native cultures, when a boy experiences an initiation ritual, he often returns with a trophy—like a pelt or a tooth from an animal he has killed—to mark his passage to manhood. The Quest Project® doesn't include a hunting component, but the transformations the boys experience are no less real. At graduation, I present each boy with a talisman that represents the work he has done and the wound he has healed, so he will never forget what he has accomplished. I also encourage parents to let their sons know that they recognize their accomplishment. It's important for parents to acknowledge that their sons have changed and are no longer the little boys they were when they first walked through my door.

The graduation ceremony is an emotional and meaningful conclusion to the sometimes intense and painful work the boys endure in The Quest Project®. It celebrates their success and reconnects them with their families as the young men they have become.

Try This at Home…

While your son may not experience this rite of passage with a group of boys, his achievement and accomplishments still deserve acknowledgment and celebration. Use your imagination—and your knowledge of your son's favorite things—to select an appropriate gift, a special meal, and of course, verbal recognition of everything he has accomplished.

Even if you have only seen small, minimal steps, trust that your son has come a long way just going through the program with you. Remember that he is young and still developing and that more changes will come. The seeds of change have been planted, and your relationship has been strengthened, so don't hold back. Take this time to celebrate your son and everything he is and will become.

The Quest Project® has been honed and developed over many years through a combination of intensive research and personal experience. One reason it works as well as it does is that parents are not present. Their absence gives the boys freedom to be honest about things that might make their parents uncomfortable or cause them pain. Another reason is that each step of the way is facilitated by a professional who can deal with any strong or uncomfortable emotions sparked by the exercises.

I understand that it's not possible for parents to replicate the exact program or expect identical results. I have shared this detailed overview of each step of the program because it represents something universal—a progression toward healing that address issues in a specific order. This makes it possible to replicate the process. Understanding the ten steps of The Quest Project® will help you understand your son's journey, and it may inspire you to find your own ways of helping your son transition to manhood.

However, the biggest gift you can give your son is the one you're giving him now, reading this book and exploring ways to be a better father and help him to become a better man. That fact that you care, you're interested in your child, and you want to be the best parent you can be will mean more to your child's development than any program can ever mean. Don't be afraid to try some of the solutions, suggestions, and exercises presented in this book, even if you're worried you might mess them up. You don't need to be perfect. You just need to be there.

My team and I are working to bring The Quest Project® into more communities, so boys across the country and around the world can benefit from the experience. If you'd like to learn more about bringing the program to your area, contact me through TheQuestProject.com.

CHAPTER 10

The Quest Project® for Men

In leading The Quest Project® for over eighteen years, I've helped thousands of boys aged eleven through nineteen to confront their pain, heal their wounds, and discover their purpose. I've helped adolescents who struggled in school, abused drugs or alcohol, or just felt hurt or lost to face the challenges of manhood feeling confident, healthy, and happy.

My passion is working with boys; but men—especially fathers—are the key to my work. That's why this past summer, while I was writing this book, I launched the first-ever Quest Project® for men.

Working with teenage boys and their issues, I naturally deal with their fathers. Sometimes I ask dads to work with me one-on-one to help them help their children, and sometimes they come to me when the work we do with their sons uncovers other issues.

These men and their sons have served as a kind of research lab for me. I've studied how the cycle of pain passes down the generational line from father to son, and I've seen how The Quest Project® helps boys break that cycle and heal their wounds. I've done it by helping boys confront their pain while providing the five things they need to become men. It only made sense to apply the same logic to healing their fathers.

With that in mind, I recruited a group of six men to participate in this new version of The Quest Project®. I reached out to men from across the economic spectrum and all different age groups, ranging from guys just entering manhood to one nearing retirement in his sixties. Some were fathers, some were stepfathers, and one was basically still a kid in a man's body.

All of these men had some experience with therapy, since they had all worked with me on previous occasions. That was important for this first time, as it was a learning experience for me, too. It was good to have already established a level of trust. These men were familiar with my style and with some of the topics we would cover. Three of the men have sons who participated in the program. I trusted this group to follow my lead, even if some of The Quest Project® exercises would take them out of their comfort zones.

Despite their differences, the group gelled almost instantly, with one exception. One of the participants, an educated, successful, middle-aged man, failed to follow the rules of the group and acted "out of integrity" (which is a professional way of saying he didn't live up to his promises). I had to ask him to leave, but the incident didn't get in the way of the rest of the group's progress. In fact, it was a catalyst that bonded the men even more tightly.

We followed the basic ten-week structure of The Quest Project®, with some modifications to accommodate the fact that I was dealing with grown men. There was no need for the sex education portion, and there was more need for work on anger and forgiveness. By the end of that ten weeks, even though they'd all done some sort of therapy before, the five men who graduated from the first-ever adult men's Quest Project® were transformed.

They were new men.

Four of those men share their stories here.

CHAPTER 11

Clint

*"I knew that no matter what I had done to deal with my dad, I'd
still have to cope with that stuff for the rest of my life."*

I had been working with Clint for a few years when I approached him about participating in the first Quest Project® for men. He was already familiar with the program. I had held a session for some students at the school where he works as a counselor, and he was impressed with the change he saw in the boys in the group. He had done some one-on-one therapy with me to work through his issues with his father.

Like so many of the men I work with, and like me, Clint grew up without the five crucial things a boy needs to become a well-adjusted man. The way his needs were unmet and the way those empty places affected him growing up were unique to Clint, yet there are aspects of his experience you may find familiar. The issues he brought to the group when he joined The Quest Project® for men included:

He lacked a healthy male role model.

Clint's father was an alcoholic and emotionally absent, and while he did not physically abuse Clint or his family, he was emotionally abusive. He cheated on Clint's mother, avoided time with the family, and was withholding and critical. He was also largely uninterested in the day-to-day business of parenting. However, this didn't change the fact that, as an adolescent boy, Clint was hardwired to look to his dad for guidance and support.

Clint: You watch TV and you see how dads are supposed to act. I knew he wasn't meeting that expectation, but I looked up to my dad. I always longed for a traditional father/son relationship. I wanted to be like him, I wanted to spend time with him, I wanted him to play ball with me, I wanted him to play video games. But he never would. If I asked, it didn't matter, it wasn't going to happen. It made me sad.

Clint was trapped in a cycle of constant rejection, where he would try to earn his father's attention, only to be pushed away. It forced Clint to think creatively about how to establish the relationship he so desperately needed with his father.

Clint: I had to work to get a few hours with him a week. I had to spend time doing things that he liked. I would sit and watch 60 Minutes *with him, or I would go mall walking with him.*

When father and son did talk, Clint found the conversations were disappointing. Occasionally his dad would offer advice, but it was usually focused on what was wrong with Clint or trying to push him into a career in business, for which Clint has no interest or aptitude. His father never really saw his son for the person he was. As a result, Clint struggled to see himself.

Clint: I didn't have any sense of what I wanted to do, who I was, what was special about me, or what I was good at. There was not a lot of ongoing, positive support. I would get a bad report card, and my dad would yell at me. He would tell me that I was an A student and it better improve. But there would be absolutely no plan or follow-up on his part, and he would act surprised when the next report card was shit.

Clint made it to high school graduation, but he got there with no idea what he wanted to do with his life. Without a role model's guidance, he was totally unprepared for the future. His driver's license said he was a legal adult, but he hadn't really grown up, because no one ever showed him how.

Clint: I was not a man. I had no idea of what the future held, and I was only living for today.

He didn't have a safe container to deal with his pain.

Adolescence is naturally a difficult time, and growing up with a critical, Absent Father sparked a lot of negative emotions for Clint to cope with as a teenager. He had no place to go and no one to talk to about his feelings. He lacked a safe "container" where he could process his pain and learn healthy ways to cope with it.

Clint: My parents got divorced. My dad moved out. My mom decided to move in with my step-dad, so my dad moved back in. Dad moved again, and I went to live with my mom and step-dad. There was no safe place. Home felt empty. I felt empty.

When you're left alone with pain, the problem is this: you have to do something with it. For adolescent boys, that often means self-medicating with alcohol or drugs. And for boys who feel worthless, it also can mean engaging in risky or dangerous behavior to get attention or self-medicating with the adrenaline rush of fear.

Clint: I would binge drink to the point of blacking out and throwing up. I would engage in risky behaviors. I would do crazy things to try to impress people.

Clint outgrew those behaviors in adulthood, but he didn't outgrow his pain. Without a safe container to process his feelings, his only option to make them go away was to continue what he knew, which was to self-medicate. So many addicted teenagers grow up to be addicted adults, because adulthood can be even more stressful than childhood. There's even more need for coping mechanisms. By the time I met Clint, he had traded the booze and crazy stunts for psycho-tropic medications, but he wasn't satisfied with their results.

Clint: I lived a number of years in a fog, taking Prozac and other stuff, that made me a different person.

He didn't know any other way to cope with his pain.

He lacked the support of a community.

Community is important, because it's where a boy is truly "seen," acknowledged, and appreciated for the person he is. This recognition helps him to identify the good in himself and to develop a self-concept that will influence his decisions as he navigates the path to adulthood. A boy's first community—his family—influences how he sees himself. Boys like Clint, who grow up in less-than-supportive families, are at a disadvantage.

Clint: My family was dysfunctional. We did not spend time together, we never vacationed or did any other type of family activity together. I acted like a clown a lot to try to get attention, and my dad let me know that he thought I was a manipulative fuck-up. He still has no idea who I am. My mom came the closest to seeing me, but my dad and brother were stuck in their worlds.

Teenage boys aren't just hardwired to seek out a role model. Many of them are also instinctively drawn to seek out community. Already labeled a "fuck-up" at home, Clint gravitated toward the only kind of community where he knew he would be accepted, and not rejected the way he was by his dad.

Clint: I just wanted to belong and ended up with the "knuckleheads." I was getting drunk, participating in vandalism, and getting suspended from school. I made a lot of cries for help, but no one ever answered those cries.

Ultimately, being a part of this community cemented Clint's self-concept as a person who couldn't do anything right.

He needed a sense of achievement, importance, and change.

One thing that helps a teenage boy rise above knucklehead-hood to find motivation and meaning is the sense that he is gaining the knowledge and experience he needs to become a man. Growing up is a huge leap into the unknown, and a boy needs an occasional reminder that things are going right, that he's making progress, that he's "getting it." Ideally, this should come from a boy's parents, especially his dad. With no sense that he's winning at the game of growing up and becoming a man, a boy will have trouble figuring out who that man is supposed to be.

Clint: My parents did not seem to care too much. They did not attend the one time I was in the spelling bee, and did not attend a single soccer game that I played in as a freshman in high school. They did not actively participate in my academic development. My dad only cared when my grades were bad, and then it was only a day of yelling. He would tell me that I was an A student, then he would tell me how stupid I was.

Other than that, Clint's parents were more than happy to leave their son to his own devices. If he received one overriding message from them, it was that they just didn't care.

Clint: They seemed to give up control as we grew up. I could run around, get drunk, shoplift, steal cars, and they had no idea.

Without any recognizable boundaries, and without any sense or assurance that he was making progress on his journey to manhood, Clint missed out on the sense of accomplishment that helps boys see themselves as strong and capable. He struggled to grow up, because no one ever made him feel like he *could* grow up.

Clint: I had absolutely no control.

He needed a ritual to mark his transformation.

Rituals are the icing on the cake of all the (sometimes painful) growth and change that happen during adolescence. Celebrating an accomplishment gives that accomplishment meaning, and it tells the boy that he's special and worthy of celebrating. This is important in the development of a boy's sense of self-worth as well as his sense of mastery and control over his life as he grows into manhood.

It probably comes as no surprise that Clint grew up without rituals or celebrations. Milestones like getting his driver's license or passing a big test weren't looked at as a reason for a change in his family's everyday routine of avoiding each other. As a result, Clint didn't experience those milestones as anything special, either.

Clint: None of those things meant a lot to me. They were expectations, nothing to celebrate.

Like the rest of Clint's childhood, there was no joy even in accomplishment.

Growing up without the support he needed in these five areas made Clint's transition from boyhood to manhood a struggle, but like most of us, he eventually got there. He grew up, built a career as a counselor, got married, and had four children of his own. But the wounds he suffered in adolescence didn't magically heal themselves. They continued to affect him years later, even as he intentionally tried to be a different kind of father and live a different kind of family life. He addressed some of his issues with me in therapy, and he made some progress, but he never found the tools to get past some of the deepest wounds his father left behind. Then he participated in The Quest Project® for men.

By design, The Quest Project® for men provides all five of those crucial things Clint missed, beginning with community. The program is structured around a community of peers who support each other as they go through the healing process. Clint became part of a group of men who, while very different, all shared a common goal—to confront and deal with their issues.

Clint: I was excited, yet apprehensive. I was ready to share, but a little nervous about the other guys in the group.

He didn't need to be. The group bonded quickly and gave Clint the support he needed to go deeper than he had in therapy.

Clint: Once things got going, I felt like we were all there together. I think they really saw me, more than most other people do. I knew that they had my back, and I had theirs. We bared our souls together, good and bad. We were there to heal, and we could only accomplish that together.

At the same time, the structure and rules of The Quest Project® gave Clint the safe container he needed to go deep and do the kind of painful work required to heal his wounds.

Clint: It was tumultuous. There were very good days and very bad days. It was scary sometimes, but I wanted to get it all out. I had been carrying it for way too long.

As the six men (including me) got to know each other, Clint found he had new role models to look to on his journey.

Clint: There were a couple of men in the group I looked up to in a lot of ways. Seeing the way they handled life's struggles was eye opening. Some of them had made some pretty bad decisions, but they were there to be held accountable and to make themselves better.

I appreciated the strength of the men in the group and their willingness to grow. I felt like we were all there to grow, and we did it together. We all learned through our shared experiences.

The Quest® Project progresses week to week, each exercise building on the one before. This provided Clint and the other group members with concrete evidence of achievement, importance, and change.

Clint: I had to face my wounds in a way that I never had before. I learned a lot about myself each week. It felt great to finally be able to see a coherent picture and to know how to approach things.

It taught me that I might have gotten screwed, but that I can be okay. I can have a good life and give my kids a good life.

So, when the ten weeks were finished and Clint joined the other group members for one final ritual—The Quest® graduation—he had reason to celebrate his accomplishment.

Clint: It was nice to acknowledge the work we had done. My wife and kids came to the graduation. It was great to have them there to share the experience with me.

Clint has moved past the pain of his childhood and the wounds his father left behind.

Clint: I carried a lot of lingering pain into adulthood. I dealt with the pain in unhealthy ways, but now I have learned to deal with the pain productively. I feel like I have the tools to deal with things now, and it is liberating. To a large extent I have been able to let go. It feels better. I feel like I can concentrate on the here and now.

And that means helping the next generation of boys—his sons—grow up healthy, happy, and whole.

Clint: I have become a better spouse and father—I have evolved as a father. I have learned a lot about myself and my place in the world. I have accepted what I can control and what I cannot.

I think that I am a great role model for my sons. I talk to them about life and what kind of men I expect them to become. I also share my mistakes and let them know how I have learned to deal with things.

My family is my tribe. We will always have each other, no matter what happens.

Clint has broken the cycle and can trust that his sons will grow into healthy, happy, productive men—like their dad.

CHAPTER 12

Larry

"The Quest, like all rituals from the ancient days to these post-modern days, is a powerful way to transmit knowledge."

At sixty-four, Larry was the oldest man to participate in The Quest Project®, which meant he brought decades of experience to the group. He also brought a unique perspective. Larry grew up in the 1960s, and half a century later, he still has a hippie's non-conformist way of looking at the world that comes through in everything he does. As a freelance artist who works alone, he spends a lot of time in his own head, analyzing everything he experiences (and even some things he doesn't!). His boundless quest for knowledge is part of the reason he ended up in my office, and then later, as part of The Quest Project® for men.

Larry found me through an interview I did for a local TV station, talking about the importance of fathers in their boys' lives, and my words hit him hard. He had lived apart from his own son for fifteen years, after separating from his wife when the boy was only two. Hearing me talk about what his son might be experiencing motivated him to act. He tracked me down, made an appointment, and came to me for help reconnecting with his now teenage son, who had moved back to St. Louis with his mom after living for some years out of state. Larry's goal was to give his son some of the things he missed growing up, before it was too late.

First, we met one-on-one, and I gave him some tips he put to use. What really lit his fire was when I told him about The Quest Project®. He was so intrigued by the idea of a guided initiation process, modeled on rituals from ancient cultures, that he enrolled his son in the program. And when he found out he could experience his own initiation ritual through The Quest Project® for men, he was all in.

Larry came to Quest® with a lot of tools many men don't have growing up. He had a close relationship with his father, at least until he reached his late teens and the generation gap of the 1960s came between them. However, his relationship with his mother was always difficult. As a result, Larry experienced a lot of pain, and he missed out on some of the five essential things a boy needs when he's growing up despite having an involved, caring father. Those were the wounds he dealt with during his time in The Quest Project® for men.

Larry started life with a healthy male role model.

Larry's dad was an active, hands-on parent who, unlike a lot of 1950s dads, actually seemed to like being with little kids. Not only did he freely offer his children guidance and support, he wasn't afraid to openly show love to Larry and his older brother and two younger sisters. That left Larry with a lot of positive feelings.

Larry: My brother and I spent a good amount of time with our father. He was always giving advice, from our earliest memory as children. When we were little boys, he playfully would tell us, "You got to be tough!" On Saturdays, we would go to his business with him, or I would go to my grandfather's shop with him.

I felt good, protected, and secure. He was a lion.

Larry was lucky to learn responsibility by going to work with his father. His dad owned his own business, an auto dealership, and as soon as Larry was old enough, he joined his father at work around the car lot. At his father's side, Larry learned the importance of hard work and doing a good job, and his dad gave him the kind of patient, step-by-step guidance he needed to master new tasks and succeed. Having the consistent presence of a strong, loving role model built Larry's work ethic and self-esteem.

Larry: I learned how to really apply myself to doing a job. That job could be cleaning up a dirty old used car, but applying everything that he taught us, he would apply that extremely mindfully, very focused, and really get that car from looking very old to looking like new. That was awesome.

Their close relationship was tested by the dramatic cultural shifts of the 1960s. Larry came of age just as the hippie movement was sweeping the country, and he got interested in art, music, new ideas, and different ways of seeing the world. His dad, a Marine veteran, could not get behind that at all. He totally disapproved of the counterculture movement, and father and son clashed. The change in his father's attitude toward him wounded Larry deeply.

Larry: I feel there was a connection missed. I wish he could have just sat down at the table and spoken the truth, you know, instead of having these barriers in the way. "I'm the father, you're the child." He didn't go to college. He did very well in business, self-made and he did well, but he was not interested in the ideal of the arts and sciences. He was more practical and could not approach that dreamy ideal.

Looking back, Larry still remembers his father positively. The experience of being so close to his dad during his boyhood and early teen years is meaningful to him. But the pain of feeling rejected by a role model, of not being appreciated for the person he was and the gifts he had, left lingering scars.

He missed the most important container a child may ever have for his pain.

As I mentioned earlier, most of Larry's pain came from his relationship with his mother. She was overwhelmed and frazzled trying to manage four kids, and she was angry and distracted most of the time. Since Mom is the first person a little boy usually turns to for comfort when he gets hurt, Larry was left with a deep wound. He couldn't turn to his mother to help him process the normal pain of growing up or the pain of her disapproval and rejection. Being deprived of that imperative support at such a young age, he never learned the tools to deal with and bounce back from things that hurt him. And since their relationship never improved, the scars only got deeper.

Larry: I think some of my wounds came from my mother. She screamed a lot when we were growing up, and she did a good share of slapping too. She didn't know how to put her attention out and compliment her children or encourage her children. Even after I grew up, she never really called me to say, like a loving mother, "Hi, how are you doing, honey? Are you doing okay? Okay, keep going. I believe in you." None of that, none, nothing.

Their mother's anger also affected Larry's older brother, who took his pain and anger out on Larry.

Larry: He abused me mentally and verbally for many years, and I never really confronted him. It doesn't go away, that kind of verbal and mental abuse. I mean, I don't think it does.

Because he never learned to deal with his pain, Larry's wounds persisted into his adult life and resulted in an inability to form connections and build a lasting, healthy relationship. He married his girlfriend when she got pregnant, but their relationship was over and he moved out before their baby boy turned three. Then, when his son was twelve, his mother moved the boy out of state, putting distance between father and son right at that pivotal point where a boy needs his dad the most.

Larry: It created separation in a big way, in a very emotional, harmful way for everyone involved, I think.

Larry was lacking in community support.

Because of the growing 1960s-fueled rift between himself and his parents, the older Larry got, the less connected he felt from the "community" of his family. Instead of seeing him as the intelligent, passionate thinker Larry knew he was, his parents saw him as just another long-haired, drug-using hippie. Larry didn't feel seen at all.

Larry: I was the brain, but they view me to this day as the fuck-up. Again, because of the negative perceptions they have of my ways, which are essentially the philosophical ways of academia and the arts and sciences. They have no idea who I really am, just their own narrow, uneducated judgment.

When their families fail them, many adolescent boys are drawn to find a community elsewhere, like in sports or some other organization. Larry wasn't interested in organized sports or organized anything. The closest he came to being part of an organization was when he played in a band as a young teen. Still, while he was never exactly "seen" by his family or a team or organization, Larry got enough support from teachers and peers that he was able to identify his talents and passions—his Gift! After high school, he pursued his dreams of higher education and became an artist.

He was helped by a strong sense of achievement, importance, and change.

The formative experience of working alongside his father as a teen gave Larry a consistent sense of achievement, importance, and change. Month after month, he was given an opportunity to learn and master new skills and was recognized when he succeeded. Where most boys experience this cycle of learning, growth, and accomplishment through sports or school, Larry learned the responsibilities of manhood directly from his dad. Accomplishing things with his father on hand to witness his growth and success helped Larry see himself as smart and capable.

Larry: I learned a lot. Working for my father was an education in business and responsibility. I felt absolutely ready for manhood.

He experienced ritual on a regular basis.

One of the most important and meaningful rituals of becoming a man is reaching a milestone, being recognized for it, and being allowed to move on to the next task—like the farm boy whose father tells him he's ready to drive the tractor. As he worked alongside his dad, Larry's early teenage years were shaped by these little rituals, and they reminded him that he was succeeding at becoming a man and that that mattered to his dad. Outside of work, his family also considered things like birthdays, holidays, and other special days as important enough to celebrate, so Larry was not deprived of ritual.

Larry: Birthdays were kind of a big deal, and we have a New Year's ritual that is celebrating and cutting the "New Year's Cake" that is an old country cultural tradition from Anatolia. When I graduated from high school, my mother and father put together a graduation party, which was expected, but nice and enjoyable.

Ritual has continued to play an important role in Larry's life, and the opportunity to take part in an initiation ritual was one of the things that drew him to The Quest Project® for men.

Larry: It really takes us back to the ancient days, where the sacred was in the mundane or the secular. The sacred was everywhere in the ancient world. And now it's separated, and we don't really talk about it.

By the time he showed up for that first meeting with me, Larry had spent a lifetime dealing with the fallout from pain he was never able to address as a child because he lacked a safe container. He had tried therapy a few times and finally reached the conclusion that he would just have to live with his wounds. When he started The Quest Project® for men, his primary goal was not healing, but learning.

Larry: As a grown-up man, I took it like, "I'm being educated. I want to observe and experience this process that this man has put together." Even though I have my wounds, I wasn't there in a broken sense, like, "Please heal me."

He was intrigued and a little nervous about the prospect of working on his issues in front of a group of strangers. However, by the end of the first meeting it was clear that, by setting clear boundaries and ground rules, The Quest Project® for men would finally provide that safe container he needed to be able to take a closer look at his pain.

Larry: I appreciated establishing the trust factor at the very first meeting. The best part was the bonding by way of the established trust, and no judgment.

Larry didn't find any role models within the group, and he doesn't feel like he served as a role model for any of the men. What mattered most to him was the support of the community of men that Quest® created.

Larry: I respect all the men and their unique perceptions of the life process. I learned from everyone I came into contact with. It opened up my perspective of that potential of connecting with men on this sacred level, this trusted level.

While Larry did not enter the program with any specific hopes for growth or change, as the weeks wore on, he couldn't help evolving as he participated in each exercise.

Larry: It was my intent to make myself present and to participate the best way I could, and to observe. I believe these changes are subtle and profound, and they may take time to latch onto the memory or the psyche.

And while he may not have expected or "set an intention" to do it, Larry ultimately found some level of healing within the rituals of The Quest Project®.

Larry: The Quest experience has certainly contributed to my belief in the mythological process of ritual and rite of passage. I wanted to experience an initiation, and I'm glad I did. It's awesome, and it's very symbolic. This is where we can potentially mend in a big way because it's symbolic, and we need symbolism in our world. All of these symbols that we look at, we know they're sacred. And that's good.

While he clearly needed to heal, what was most important to Larry, and what brought him to my office in the first place, was improving his relationship with his son—especially since he missed the beginning of his son's teenage years.

Larry: I'm doing all I can to reconnect with him, and it's taking a while.

Larry always tried to be supportive of his son, even when distance made it impossible. The Quest Project® for men helped Larry connect to his son on a man-to-man level by giving him a new kind of insight into what kinds of things his son is experiencing as he grows up. This has enabled Larry to be there for his son in a more powerful, purposeful way.

Larry: It's made me even more open to my son's feelings and in his everyday quest. We're moving forward very well together. I've really learned a lot from him—how to be more sensitive and more neutral.

When it was time for graduation from The Quest Project®, Larry brought his son to experience this final ritual with him. Because, in a way, his son is what brought him to Quest® in the first place.

Larry: I wanted him to witness this event for his knowledge, this whole discovery. The Quest Project® initially was intended for my son. The subliminal ocean-current must have signed me up.

Whatever actually brought Larry to my door, I'm very happy it happened. He healed his own pain and broke the cycle of pain in his family by learning to be there for his only child.

Larry: My relationship with my son has changed since The Quest Project® and will change even more. I need to do more and put more emphasis on my son's awesome existence.

That's what being a Good Dad is all about.

CHAPTER 13

Russ

"When I was younger, my dad was a hero. Then as I got to be 15,
16, 17, I started realizing that he wasn't that fantastic…"

Every individual's story is unique. Still, some people's unique stories are more remarkable than others. Russ's story is one of those.

When I first met him more than a decade ago, Russ was looking for help with issues ranging from anger management and domestic violence to drug and alcohol abuse. We worked together off and on, in one-on-one therapy and in my men's groups, and two of his three sons participated in The Quest Project®. When I launched the men's version, I thought Russ would benefit from the group, and I invited him to join.

Russ's father was absent when he was little. His parents split up before he was a year old, and he spent his early childhood with an uncaring mother and an abusive stepfather. At age thirteen, he moved in with his dad, and he spent his teenage years with a father figure who was available and involved in his life.

In most cases, this would have given Russ an advantage when it came to the five kinds of support a boy needs to become a healthy man. Unfortunately, Russ's father lived by a different set of values than most of us, and the line between right and wrong in Russ's family was blurred. Support for Russ often encouraged bad behavior instead of good, and in the end, the lessons he learned from his father did not prepare him to survive and thrive as a productive member of society. Instead, they prepared him for a life of hardship.

His primary role model was present and engaged, but flawed.

As a little boy, Russ idolized his father. He didn't see much of him during the school year, but in the summer he would escape his stepfather's abuse and his mother's indifference by staying at grandparents' farm. There, he finally got to spend some time with his dad. His grandparents did most of the "parenting," and his dad wasn't always around, but to Russ, that just made him seem that much more awesome.

Russ: When I was little it was like, "My dad travels around," kind of like Ricky Bobby. I always thought he was a stuntman or a race car driver or something like that, because I always saw wrecked cars in the driveway.

Moving in with his father at thirteen, Russ gained a role model at the exact moment he was biologically driven to need one. Unlike his stepfather, Russ's dad was interested in spending time with his son, and he provided a regular, consistent presence in his life.

Russ: He taught us how to do everything, hunt, have fun, he taught us how to do all that stuff. He didn't miss a beat as far as that in the parent part. Every kid in my neighborhood loved him. My dad was like the originator of "no kid left behind." I remember him standing on the front porch in his underwear with a gun behind his back talking to some bikers, but the neighbors still let my dad take their kids camping and shit like that. I couldn't believe that.

Growing up with an active role model who took the time to support his son and teach him what it meant to be a man provided Russ with a flawed foundation. The lessons Russ's father taught his son were more about taking risks and breaking the law than about mastering the skills a boy needs to succeed and become a productive member of society.

Russ: It was more like living with a big brother. We would go out and steal our Christmas tree every year. We would drink together, and I was only thirteen. I was pretty much his chauffeur. I learned to drive when I was thirteen, because he was too drunk to drive.

He always told me, "Boy, there is a difference between fucking up and fucking off." But nothing was ever clear. It was always a riddle.

School was not a priority in Russ's family, so he dropped out in tenth grade and went to work with his dad. They spent their days working on cars together, drinking together, and stealing cars together. But as Russ grew older and stronger, father and son clashed more and more over the way Russ's dad treated his stepmother.

Russ: I became the peace keeper. I started having to be the parent between the two of them, because they would be knocking the shit out of each other, and I had two baby brothers I was looking out for. I was constantly getting in trouble, or the cops were getting called, because I was either restraining her or restraining him. They got pissed off because I wasn't taking their side, and they'd kick me out. I was living on the street for a while.

One of those fights resulted in Russ's dad calling the police, and Russ wound up in juvenile hall. Suddenly, the dad who always had his back, didn't.

Russ: I actually expected him to come in guns blazing to get me out of juvenile hall. I remember him sitting with the judge calling me "incorrigible." That was the first time that I ever heard my dad really talk bad about me or say something about me other than, "Go fuck yourself." It was the first time I ever remember my dad saying something that hurt my feelings. He lost his credibility.

Russ never had a safe container where he could process his pain.

Russ spent his early years with a mother who failed to protect him from his step-father's abuse.

Russ: I felt betrayal from my mother. She didn't have my back, she didn't take care of me like she was supposed to, and I had to learn how to take care of myself.

The abuse stopped when he moved in with his father, but the wounds from his mother's neglect remained. And there was no place in Russ's father's world for a boy to process that kind of pain in a healthy way. Russ's dad was tough, and Russ was expected to be tough. That's how he was taught to show the world he was a man.

Russ: It was always hit first, ask questions later.

Instead of coping with his pain, Russ self-medicated with alcohol and drugs. He was prone to anger and violence, which led to stints in group homes and juvenile detention facilities. And all of that just enhanced his tough-guy image.

Russ: I remember you had to sleep with your pants on the door. I was thinking, "Why would anybody want to kill themselves with their pants?" I wasn't in that state of mind where I was worried about taking my life. I wasn't sad or upset; it was just an experience. I was just doing my time until I could get out. I knew my friends were going to think I was a hero. I'd be like, "I just got out of juvenile detention," and they'd be like, "You're kickass."

Under his ass-kicking exterior, Russ never learned a healthy way to cope with his pain. His anger issues and substance abuse problems followed him into adulthood.

Russ's community was supportive, but it supported the wrong things.

Teenage Russ was surrounded by family and friends who encouraged the same choices and behaviors that limited his options and sent him down a destructive path. No one in Russ's life presented him with options beyond a life of petty crime. No one helped him discover his natural intelligence and other gifts or encouraged him to pursue a more positive path. Russ's community saw him as both "the fuckup" and "the enforcer," but in his community, that was a good thing. That meant respect.

Russ: I did the crazy stuff, and they enjoyed it. I used to climb the electrical towers down by my girlfriend's house. I remember one time it was a windy day, and they bet me that I wouldn't drop a match and wait until the count of ten to stomp it out, because it was so windy. I counted to ten and burned up half of the local ballpark.

In Russ's teenage world, being tough and fearless earned more respect than being an A student or a conscientious, responsible worker. Russ's community shaped him to be tough and fearless.

Russ experienced growth, importance, and change…again, in all the wrong places.

How many kids get to drink beer and drive a car at thirteen—with their father's blessing? Nothing was off-limits to Russ, and he grew up confident, strong, and capable of learning new things and meeting new challenges. The problem was, the skills Russ mastered on his journey to manhood were the same skills that would eventually derail him.

Russ: I worked with my dad and drank and stole cars. He taught me how, and I expanded on it on my own. I always wanted him to be proud of me. There was always something happening, we were always doing something, whether it was right or wrong, we were doing it.

Russ may have felt grown up and accomplished when he reached adulthood, but he lacked many of the skills he needed to survive in the real world—a world without crime, that is!

The rituals in Russ's life followed the same counterproductive pattern.

From the moment he moved in with his father, Russ was unknowingly on a path that would ultimately land him in jail, with unhealthy rituals reinforcing every step in that journey. These weren't the kind of rituals most fathers share with their sons. Birthday parties or getting a driver's license or graduating high school weren't a big deal in Russ's family. His ritual and celebration was about taking risks and breaking rules.

Russ: Dad use to take us out to steal our Christmas tree every year. I've never taken my kids to steal a Christmas tree, but God I wanted to—just because that was such a fun thing when I was a kid.

Russ's rituals were tied up with the experiences he shared with his dad and his brothers—the fun of making their own rules, of getting away with things other people don't, of feeling free from the laws that constrain most human beings. Those things gave Russ's life meaning, but it wasn't meaningful in the real world. The kinds of accomplishments that gave Russ his confidence and self-esteem, like stealing cars and winning fights and holding his liquor, were problematic at best and illegal at worst. The good feelings he got from those actions could not carry over into his adult life. And by the time he was a legal adult, Russ's journey reached its logical conclusion.

Russ: I went to prison. That's what happens.

Despite his rough ride, Russ still considers himself lucky. He credits prison with saving his life—in jail, he was able to quit drugs and alcohol, and he made a vow to live the rest of his life and raise his four children on the right side of the law.

Russ struggled to be a good husband and a good father. He was never given the tools he needed to heal from his childhood wounds, and he was unprepared for how difficult building a "good" life can be for anyone, especially a person with a criminal record. He was headed toward his third divorce and still struggling with the issues from his tumultuous childhood when he joined The Quest Project® for men.

Despite coming to the program from a very different place than most of the other participants, he found acceptance within the community.

Russ: I could relate to everyone in different ways with their similar circumstances.

The group provided the safe container Russ had been missing all his life, where he could finally begin to deal with the pain that caused him so many problems. But at first, the process was difficult.

Russ: It's hard to dig out, because you bury most of it, and you aren't aware of how it affects your day-to-day life.

At first, it's kind of intimidating, especially when you see somebody get down on the floor and start beating the shit out of a pillow and screaming. You're thinking, "What the fuck is going on here? What am I doing? Does this shit really work?"

Before long, Russ discovered that, strange as it might have seemed, the exercises in the program work. The exercises helped Russ understand his emotions and the wounds behind some of the things he had done. He realized that he wasn't a "bad person," that there were actual reasons he did what he did and made the choices he made. For the first time, Russ saw himself and his issues in a new way.

Russ: I felt relieved and more focused on what the real problems are and not the reaction to the problem.

Week by week, Russ was able to uncover and address his pain in a structured, systematic way. And every week, he was inspired to get better.

Russ: There were always new things to be aware of and things to push myself toward. When I was feeling like I wasn't getting anywhere, or I wasn't doing anything, something would happen, and I would already be ahead of it, because I had learned it.

The support of the group was instrumental to Russ's ability to see himself as capable of so much more.

Russ: I feel they saw what I can be from working with the broken pieces. I could see them "feel" what I was saying and knew it was helping them with their own work.

Russ's experience in The Quest Project® has also changed the way he parents his boys.

Russ: The hardest thing about being a single dad, parent, is follow-through. It's a whole lot easier now that they live with me, but it's still hard, because you don't want to stifle them. I'm more aware of their moods and actions. I ask more (and they provide more) about what they are doing in school and in life. I'm honest with them—I made all the mistakes, and they know all my secrets, so they can learn from them.

Today, Russ is carrying on some of the positive traditions he learned from his father, like providing his boys with a strong foundation of love and support. But he's also breaking the cycle that prevented him from becoming a productive member of society. Unlike his father, Russ is giving his boys the right kind of guidance, providing consequences and boundaries and his own example of how a troubled person can turn his life around.

Russ: I was the kind of person who would hit everybody first and then ask questions. I had so much anger because of everything that happened to me in my younger days that it was easier to just knock everybody out and then deal with those consequences, because that problem was easier than what I had to actually face.

Now, it takes a lot to bring a rise out of me. I can let shit roll off of me, or I just deal with it in a different way. Instead of just getting angry and reacting, I think before I react.

More importantly, The Quest Project® helped him face and heal his deepest wound and finally forgive himself and his father.

Russ: As a kid, I thought, "My dad's awesome." I still think my dad's awesome, but he did a lot of fucked up shit. I can't believe that he even survived.

Quest® also gave Russ new and important tools he was never taught as a child—things like anger management, conflict resolution, and how to be a healthy male and father figure. Finally, by having a chance to see himself through other people's eyes, he learned that, underneath it all, he's not so different from them. Just like his brothers in The Quest Project®, Russ has hope for a better, more productive future.

Russ: Despite who you are and where you come from, you can push through adversity and achieve good things. The only way up is by working on the wound, which means processing it in a healthy way and environment.

When the ten weeks were over and Russ participated in the graduation ritual with his ex-wife and his former stepdaughter looking on, it really was a new beginning for him.

Russ: It was fantastic to acknowledge and be acknowledged by a group of men trying to be better men.

I'm happy to have been part of providing Russ with a new lease on life, and I hope that he will continue to push for the good things he—and his boys—deserve.

Russ can feel confident today that he is, in fact, a better man.

CHAPTER 14

Craig

*"I was not confident around my Dad, not pins and needles, but I
didn't feel like I could do much right."*

The launch of the men's version of The Quest Project® happened at the exact moment Craig needed it. I had first met him more than fifteen years before; in the aftermath of his first divorce, I helped him develop a stronger sense of self and learn how to be the best single dad he could be to his twin boys. Unfortunately, despite his best efforts, Craig's second marriage also fell apart just as I was putting together The Quest Project® for men.

I thought the support of a community of men might help him finally get to the bottom of the pain that was still holding him back. His twins had been through The Quest Project® years before, so he had personally witnessed the results, and he was happy to sign on. He even enrolled his son from his second marriage in the boys' program that ran at the same time. That meant father and son essentially went through Quest® simultaneously.

Of all the men in the group, Craig is probably the best example of someone who had a "normal" childhood. He describes his father as "a good guy," and while his mother suffered from depression, the rest of his extended family offered him a lot of love and support. After his parents divorced when he was sixteen, he stayed with his father. His dad was present in his everyday life throughout his trying teenage years.

Unfortunately, while Craig's father was a good guy, he wasn't an especially good *father*. That chain of knowledge I mentioned earlier that passes down from father to son had been broken when Craig's dad was a boy.

Craig: My dad's father died when he was very young, so he didn't know how to be a dad.

Having a father who did not know how to parent him in a positive way was enough to deprive Craig of some of the five things a boy needs to grow into a healthy man.

His dad was a strong role model, but Craig felt like his father looked down on him.

Craig's dad was like a father right out of a TV sitcom. He worked hard and provided a stable life for his family, did chores around the house, played softball with his work buddies on the weekends, and was liked by just about everyone in the community. This gave Craig a solid role model he felt good about.

Craig: He was my Dad, so I was proud to be with him.

The problem was that modeling responsible behavior was the only thing Craig's father really knew how to provide his son. When it came to giving him the individual attention a teenage boy needs from his father, and the guidance that comes with it, Craig's dad was more of an Absent Father.

Craig: I didn't spend a lot of one-on-one time with my dad growing up. We did a lot of things as a family, but one-on-one time was fairly minimal.

Because he grew up without his own father's guidance, Craig's dad did not know how to teach Craig the lessons a boy is supposed to learn. Parenting consisted of pointing out what his son was doing wrong. Though he tried to be helpful and guide his son towards success, the constant stream of negativity and "don't-be" messages made Craig feel like a failure.

Craig: I didn't really have a sense of who or what he wanted me to be. He was critical, highly critical, and not much interested in doing things with me.

That kind of rejection from the most important person in his life led Craig to grow up with low self-esteem.

Craig: He told me I was stupid a lot. Anything I was doing was stupid; he was not supportive. It created a situation where I did not feel that I had much value. I never felt all that good about myself.

Without a role model to help him discover his passion or his Gift, Craig drifted through much of high school. He dreamed of becoming an Air Force pilot, but without his father's support and encouragement, he didn't take any steps toward making that dream a reality. However, because he was hardwired to follow the example of a responsible man set by his father, Craig managed to straighten himself out in time to graduate high school and go on to technical college.

Craig: The only thing that I really knew in life was that I was going to be expected to take care of my family and that I was going to need a job, so I went to school.

He went on to a successful career, but his low self-esteem persisted into his adult life.

His mother's depression deprived him of a safe container to deal with his pain.

Before his teen years, Craig had a good relationship with his mother. Where his father was distant and critical, his mother was supportive. But as he got older, his mother fell deeper into depression, and that relationship slipped away.

Craig: My mom checked out of home life when I was around fourteen. She was heavily sedated on some sort of prescribed medication. She divorced my dad when I was sixteen. I stayed with my dad mainly because I didn't want to change schools, but also because I felt sorry for my dad and was really pissed at my mom.

Craig couldn't talk with his father about the pain of losing his mother. They didn't have the kind of relationship where Craig felt comfortable opening up about his feelings. Besides, as much as he was hurting, he figured his father probably felt worse. So he turned to the place most teenage boys turn when they aren't getting the support they need.

Craig: My friends became my family. While we still did family things, I pretty much withdrew from the family and hung out with my friends.

He developed the same coping strategy as many teenagers who don't have a safe container to process their pain.

Craig: I smoked a lot of weed and drank.

Craig's self-medication didn't develop into an addiction, but he never learned a healthy way to process his pain. The wounds from the loss of his mother and his father's rejection never healed, but instead, followed him into adulthood.

Craig: I was never really sure in my manhood and felt that I could get by on just being a nice guy—an insecure one, but a nice guy. It was only after my first failed marriage, when I went into counseling with Clay, that I learned about myself as a man and areas that I really needed to mature and grow.

Craig gravitated to a community that held him back.

A boy's primary community—the first people to "see him" and give him a sense of who he is as a person—is his family. And Craig's family gave him a very clear and distinct picture of who he was.

Craig: I was a nice kid, and I know my family saw that, but I think they thought I was a fuckup and wouldn't amount to much.

Their definition became Craig's identity. He wasn't interested in sports and never got involved in any extracurricular activities. He wasn't motivated to try hard in school, so he skated by as a solid C student and attracted little attention from his teachers. Instead, he found his home in the one community where he knew he would not be rejected.

Craig: I had a lot friends, but my group was mainly outcasts. We were tight but felt like it was us against the world. Interestingly enough and in retrospect, none of the guys I hung around with had a good relationship with their father.

Fortunately, the responsibility Craig learned from his father came into play when he realized the community he had chosen was not the best place for him.

Craig: One of my close friends in school got arrested, and one of my other close friends dropped out of high school. It caused me to ask, "What am I doing?" That's when I decided I was smarter than that.

Ultimately, Craig was able to decide on his own that he no longer wanted to be seen as a fuckup, but he was ready to reach for something better. He determined that he had an aptitude for technical work (his Gift) and directed himself toward a career he would enjoy. However, he still felt like no one saw the "real Craig"—in fact, even he didn't know who the "real Craig" was.

Craig's childhood was missing a strong sense of achievement, importance, and change.

Like a lot of middle-class boys without a strong interest in sports, Craig participated in a wide range of activities, some of which provided him with a sense of accomplishment.

Craig: I was an altar boy at church and really liked that, played clarinet and was elected to the honors band, which I was very proud of. I was a Scout, was pretty good at bowling and won a lot of trophies...but nothing of consequence.

None of these accomplishments was enough to give Craig a sense of mastery over his life as he grew up. Nothing he did felt like a step toward manhood and learning the skills he would need.

Craig: Stuff just happened. I never really learned about taking control of your life and destiny until much later.

Ritual played a role in Craig's life, but not in ways that were focused on him.

Some of Craig's best childhood memories involve the rituals he enjoyed with his extended family.

Craig: We always had the family over for birthdays, we always got together for the big holidays, Christmas, Easter, Memorial Day, July 4th, Labor Day, etc. It was something I looked forward to and always enjoyed it. I really liked my cousins a lot.

Craig received no recognition for his individual achievements—his interests and accomplishments weren't "high-profile" enough to earn special attention when everyone was so focused on their own lives.

Craig: We used to go to McDonald's as a treat when I got good grades in school. That was about the extent of it.

Craig was able to recognize some of his own achievements and found ways to celebrate them on his own, despite his parents.

Craig: Getting my driver's license was a big deal to me, and graduation was an accomplishment. I don't feel like they were minimalized by my parents, but there wasn't anything beyond what I felt was a normal response.

That "normal response" from Craig's family fits well with his basically "normal" childhood. He didn't enter adulthood crippled by depression or saddled with addiction after a childhood of abuse and dysfunction. He wrestled with the unresolved mental bumps and scrapes left over from his childhood. Like most men, and maybe even like you, Craig was able to function despite the things he didn't get from his parents. He was able to break the cycle of pain on his own, by making a conscious decision to be the best father he possibly could. His first marriage broke up when his twins were only four—that was the beginning of our work together, and it has paid off.

Craig: They got the benefit of good "dadding." My sons are not necessarily having any regret over the life that they didn't have...if you talk to them, they have very good memories of when they were little, the time that we spent together. That one-on-one time with me when they were little, they've been affected by that positively.

Craig's life had a lot of good in it—his career was thriving, and he threw himself into fatherhood, coaching wrestling teams and enjoying the process of getting to know his sons on a deeper level, shaping them into good men.

Craig: I started coaching to be close to my oldest boys after divorce from their mother and found it was something I was pretty good at. It helped us develop a bond and gave us something in common that carried us through the years. Alone time in the car going to early practices or long trips for sports tournaments have been great times together, leading to great discussion. It truly is incredible.

But all the love and accomplishment in the world can't heal the wounds of childhood, and Craig was not an exception to that rule. Those wounds hung around and continued to come between Craig and the peace of mind he deserved.

When Craig and his second wife divorced after fifteen years of marriage, he was shocked to learn that everyone in his family, including his kids, were relieved. They all—even her own son! —felt Craig's wife treated him so badly that he was better off without her. Why would a nice, successful man like Craig choose a partner who treated him so badly, especially after he chose wrong the first time? He was ready to discover what was behind those issues when The Quest Project® for men began.

Craig found the program to be the safe container he needed. It allowed him to dig deep and work on his wounds among other men experiencing the same. For the first time, he was part of a brotherhood he could trust and rely on.

Craig: It was a good group of men. We held each other accountable and were like brothers in helping each other grow and console each other when we were down. It was something I really looked forward to. I loved it.

That community gave Craig the support he needed, not only by helping him work through his pain, but by seeing him as the good, responsible, successful man he was and validating that.

Craig: I really appreciated being around other men that I could relate to who were going through similar things that I was. Having these guys around, listening to their stories, being able to give feedback and comfort was very rewarding. I was not rejected or shamed or made to feel like a fuckup. I have no doubt the guys saw who I really was. They saw a nice guy, a funny, accountable, and loyal guy who wanted to better understand himself and be a better man.

As the weeks went by, Craig became more confident, as he finally learned to understand the wounds from his childhood and how to cope with them and grow beyond them.

Craig: I can't tell you how compelling it was to learn about the deep pain I had inside of me and how that affected who I am and how I behave. Knowing these things allows you to let go, to grow and mature. I understand so many things about myself that I really never knew or understood. I am so much better equipped now to deal with challenges and can now recognize the signs that caused me to lash out previously and potentially create more problems in my life than solutions.

Now I feel that I am a much better communicator, am very confident in expressing my needs and not taking on other people's issues as if my needs were the cause.

At the graduation ritual, Craig celebrated his achievement.

Craig: I feel it is one of my most important accomplishments personally.

And he celebrated in the way that was most meaningful to him—sharing the occasion with his youngest son, who was also graduating Quest®.

Craig: That's all that mattered. I did not invite anyone else.

Today, Craig feels more at peace, more in control of his destiny, and more prepared to move forward and live a full and happy life.

Craig: I really want to be the best man I can possibly be, so I really enjoyed learning about what makes me tick, gaining tools and processes to work through challenges in relationships and work. All of these have been wonderful experiences.

And while he has always worked hard toward being a Good Dad, his time in Quest® has made him much stronger. And being able to share the experience with his youngest son has been the icing on the cake.

Craig: We both know we have been through the program and are better equipped to deal with issues and challenges. Knowing my son has these tools has made me more comfortable in challenging him when he needs to be challenged, and I think it has enabled him to better communicate with me what he needs. I feel that we are closer now than we were before—even though we were already close.

If every father and son could have a relationship like that, I believe the world would be a better place.

That's why I do the work I do.

CHAPTER 15

Moving Forward

The fathers who completed the first Quest Project® for men with me provide a good snapshot of the state of manhood circa 2018. Some of their challenges may resonate with you, while others may be completely different from your experiences. However, these four very different individuals gained a common understanding of their experiences as men. They joined forces to help each other uncover wounds they had carried since childhood, and they learned to heal from them. They also gained tools to help them break the cycle of pain and be present for their sons in ways their fathers were never there for them.

It's your turn to do the same.

Throughout this book, I hope you gained some insight into why you are the way you are, both as a father and as a man. I hope you picked up some understanding of the pain you've been carrying, along with some tools to help you heal from that pain and forgive yourself for your mistakes. I also hope you've gained a deeper understanding of what your son is experiencing as he navigates his teenage years, and what he needs from you to grow up healthy and happy and reach his full potential as a man.

The journey may not be easy. Your son is coming of age in the era of *#metoo* and school shootings, a time when the nature of masculinity is being scrutinized, questioned, and sometimes demonized, and "the way things have always been," for better or worse (and likely a little of both), is under attack.

Your job as a Good Dad is to provide solid ground for your son in an uncertain world.

I believe that masculinity is not a problem to be eliminated, but a gift to be nurtured, grown, and ultimately celebrated. You, Dad, are the key to helping your son discover how to develop and use his unique brand of masculinity to grow into the best man he can be.

You do that by setting healthy boundaries for your son and natural consequences to encourage him to respect those boundaries.

You do that by giving your son the five kinds of support he needs to grow into a healthy man: a healthy male role model (you); a safe container for his pain; the support of a community; a sense of growth, importance, and change; and rituals to celebrate his accomplishments and give them—and his life—meaning.

You do that by setting aside three to five hours every week to spend with your son one on one, providing guidance, listening to what he has to say, helping him with his problems, offering advice, and just hanging out and enjoying this amazing human being you've created.

And if you find that either you or your son needs help navigating some of these challenges, reach out for the assistance you need to make sure your son reaches his full potential.

Helping your son discover how to develop and use his unique brand of masculinity to grow into the best man he can be may even mean discovering your own unique brand of masculinity.

Raising a teenager is a challenge, but it's also an opportunity to be part of the solution to the crisis that's been destroying our boys. By becoming a present, active, engaged father, you will be doing your part to break the cycle of pain that has led to this crisis point. You will be part of raising the healthy, capable generation of men the world needs to tackle the challenges of the future.

It's a big job. I know you can do it.

Afterword

I've mentioned my own difficult childhood and the struggles that came out of that. I've explained that I work with boys who are hurting, because I was a boy who hurt. Before I leave you, I'd like to share more of the details of my story, so you can understand where I come from and why I've chosen the work that I do.

I grew up the oldest of three kids in a working-class family in suburban St. Louis. Our dad had been in the Marines and became a blue-collar worker. He was an alcoholic Absent Father who physically and mentally abused my mother, my siblings, and me. Much of my childhood was spent moving back and forth between our home and our grandparents' house or sleeping in the car, as my mother packed up the kids and left my father over and over again. I grew up with very little support or stability, carrying the painful, damaging knowledge that I was not a priority.

Unlike many of the boys I work with, I wasn't the kid who got in trouble. I didn't act out, because I feared my father and his rages. My survival mechanism was to avoid provoking him at all costs. I worked hard to keep my siblings in line, and I spent a tremendous amount of energy flying under the radar.

Because of my PTSD and my unstable home environment, I did poorly in school. I grew up with a strong sense that no matter what I did or how hard I tried, I would never be good enough.

Looking back, I realize that I was lucky that I was afraid to get into trouble, although this is not uncommon in children who do not feel loved or wanted. I lived with fear every single day. I was more at the quiet and unhappy end of the spectrum than the boy who is loud, acts out, and calls attention to himself.

When I was a freshman in high school, I told my father I wanted to be a doctor. His response was, "Forget it—you're not smart enough." He never asked me what I wanted to do with my life, except to remind me that all the factory jobs—the only work he apparently thought I was capable of—were going away, so I'd better figure something out. I grew up without any sense of direction, except away from the insanity of my family.

To escape the insanity, I began to self-medicate with alcohol. I turned to girls for the love and attention I didn't get from my parents. I became obsessed with the way I looked, to the point of becoming narcissistic.

My parents finally split up for good during my senior year in high school. In an attempt to "go out with a bang," my mom burned our house down. My four-month-old puppy died in the fire, along with a lifetime of childhood memories, some good and some bad. Soon after that, my girlfriend—my first love—broke up with me.

I graduated high school damaged and lost.

I attempted college. But with no real direction and no idea what I wanted from the experience or what might interest me, I drifted. Eventually, I dropped out and joined the Air Force. It saved my life.

Even as I reached my twenties, I still searched for a male role model. My toxic relationship with my own father had deteriorated to the point where he actually attempted to kill me, strangling me with his bare hands the week before my first wedding. I was twenty years old, and my father was still abusing me.

The military was like another father to perform for and please, except this father was consistent and rewarded me when I did well. That consistency, combined with the knowledge that I could perform to somebody's expectations, guided me to manhood. I excelled, my confidence grew, and when my tour of duty was over,

I went back to college and got an engineering degree. I was invited to become a commissioned officer in the Air National Guard, on track to become a general.

On the outside, I was a success. But inside I was still a mess. I still drank to numb the pain from childhood wounds that never healed. I still looked to women to provide me with the love I didn't get growing up. I wound up with two failed marriages, because I could never get enough.

I might have continued to live that way forever, if I hadn't lost my job in the military.

Losing my military career was more than just losing my job—it meant losing my entire identity as a military man. My role models, my community, and all the tasks and rituals that defined my life and gave it meaning were ripped away in a single moment.

That sent me into such a deep depression, I finally had to reach for help. Getting that help enabled me to do what I do today.

One of the highlights of The Quest Project® is the night I help the boys discover their Gift—the thing that is unique to them that gives their life purpose. It took me more than thirty years to learn that, in a strange way, the pain I endured and the abuse I suffered as a boy is *my* Gift. It gives me insight into the wounds that other people, especially boys and men, carry with them every day. It inspired me to learn how to help them heal those wounds and live lives filled with joy and peace—the lives they were meant to live.

I guess God did have a good reason for putting me through so much pain when I was a boy.

And for that, I am grateful.

Dr. Clayton Lessor, LPC, Capt. USAF, (Ret)

March, 2018

Index

A

B

C

D

E

F

G

H

healing process, 56–57
help, when to call for, 17
Hero's Journey, 85
homicide/violence, 22
    warning signs of, 18–19
house rules, setting out, 13, 21

I

in-patient programs, 23
incapacitated fathers, 30–31
industrial revolution, 26, 51
initiation rituals, 68, 88–89, 103–104, 110
    and anger work, 82
    See also coming of age

J

Jason Foundation, 18
joy, after anger work exercise, 82–83

L

Larry, 103–111
Lawlis, Dr. Frank, *The ADD Answer: How To Help Your Child Now*, 36
love, 86

M

manhood
    boys impressions of, 47
    and responsibility, 48
    transitioning into, 48–49, 51, 53, 59–60
    See also coming of age
masculinity, 1, 3, 133–134
medication, for ADD/ADHD, 35–38
mental health professionals, involving, 17–18
milestones, 60
military, 58–61, 138–139
mothers, 3, 9, 25, 27, 29–30, 41, 43, 55, 64
    Craig's, 123, 125–126, 137
    Larry's, 105–106
    Russ's, 113, 115–116

N

natural consequences, 12–15, 21
    See also consequences
negative emotions, 78–79

P

pain, 79–80
    containers for, 50–51, 58, 67, 109
    fathers', 56, 80
parent meetings, 77
    and the Quest Project®, 73
Parental Alienation Syndrome, 28
peer communities, 98–99
peer groups, 126
    supportive, 52
peer pressure, 42, 96
    and destructive behavior, 47
peers, support from, 73
perpetual adolescence, 44–45
police, 21–23
    when to call, 17–18

The Quest Project Manifesto

As a man among many, I will stand for something.

I will be strong when the world asks me to be strong.

And soft when the world needs me to be soft.

I will make progress, not excuses. I will earn the right to manhood. I will re-earn it.

I will respect women. And I will support my brothers.

We will confront our trauma. Deal with it. Move past it. Grow.

We won't settle for the immaturity of boyhood, nor the toxicity imposed by society.

We will own our shit and strike the drum of manhood with consistency and resolve.

We will be ourselves, and prove ourselves.

This is my journey. This is our quest.

Generation of men.

THE QUEST▲ PROJECT

This Isn't Your Grandpa's Therapy.
It's a Modern-Day Rite of Passage.

The Quest Project is a 10-week, intensive group therapy program that has helped more than 2,000 boys and families.

Quest's group dynamic breaks down traditional counseling barriers, starting at week one. In 90-minute sessions, each participant works with others in his age-group to build character, sift through trauma, forgive the past, take responsibility, look to the future, and essentially…become men.

Think of it as a modern-day rite of passage. Without the bear-hunt.

All boys need improved tools in their Emotional Toolkit:

- Earning and establishing trust
- Uncovering past hurts and wounds
- Processing anger
- Conflict resolution
- Identifying individual strengths and unique gifts
- Exploring forgiveness, values, and relationships
- Establishing a purpose and goals for the future

Learn more at TheQuestProject.com.